A D V A N C E D
POOL

Techniques and Strategies for Mastering the Game

GEORGE FELS

CONTEMPORARY
BOOKS
A TRIBUNE NEW MEDIA COMPANY

Library of Congress Cataloging-in-Publication Data

Fels, George.
    Advanced pool : techniques and strategies for mastering the game /
George Fels.
        p.   cm.
    Includes index.
    ISBN 0-8092-3321-5 (alk. paper)
    1. Pool (Game)   I. Title.
GV893.F45   1995
794.7'3—dc20
                             95-24517
                              CIP

Cover design by Laurie Liebewein
Interior design by Kim Bartko

A portion of the material in this book was published previously in *Mastering Pool*.

Published by Contemporary Books, Inc.
Two Prudential Plaza, Chicago, Illinois 60601-6790
Manufactured in the United States of America
International Standard Book Number: 0-8092-3321-5
10   9   8   7   6   5   4   3   2   1

For Dale Fels,
who accepted pool as my one and only mistress

Contents

Introduction

Let's begin with a simple analogy: Suppose, for the sake of discussion, that you know absolutely nothing about chess. It should take no more than 20 to 30 minutes for you to memorize and recite all the moves that the various pieces may legally make. But that ability will still leave you totally helpless when it comes to playing the game.

This book's cover and title promise you information about pool, not chess, but in this instance the two games are not dissimilar, especially when it comes to instruction. Most of pool's modest bibliography has strived to teach you how to shoot balls into pockets—seemingly the object of the game.

Except it isn't. It's a *requirement* of the game, but *pool's real object is to stop a cue ball someplace.* The sooner you acknowledge that subtlety, the sooner you're on your way to some vast improvements in your game. After all, pocketing a single ball is all but irrelevant unless one ball is all you need to win. You win in this game by consistently stringing shots together, pocketing one ball while stopping the cue ball someplace advantageous to pocketing another. And to do that, you have to do more than just knock balls in. You have to play a game. Correctly.

That's what this book is all about. At the time my first book, *Mastering Pool*, was published in the late '70s, it was the first to address advanced play in any depth. The lion's share of worthwhile conceptual information (not mere tips for a specific table layout, but the ideas, theories, and abstractions that you can take to the table however the balls lie) that first appeared in *Mastering Pool* is here, much enriched by what I've learned in the generation since. This book will *not* instruct you on how to take your stance, form your bridge, aim, or execute your stroke; almost every other pool book and most teachers do that, and some do it well. This book assumes you have the game's fundamentals in tow to the extent that you can make some shots in a row and are able to talk instead about how the game is played. Rather than dwelling on what you should do, this book focuses on *why* you should do it—and instructs you not in the pocketing of balls, but in the correct playing of the game. The emphasis will be on Straight Pool, not because of that game's popularity (which sadly seems to have slipped among advanced players) but because it's still the best single teaching tool for all other pool games.

The truth is, all pool is largely a mental endeavor, rated by its experts to be as much as 80 percent mental. Your physical range of motion in any given stroke will generally be not much more than 8 inches or so; all that's really supposed to move is your stroking forearm and your eyeballs. Your objective is to roll 5-ounce balls a few feet, often a few inches, on smooth level cloth, so no killer strength is needed or even useful. Yes, you do require a certain level of hand/eye coordination, a skill needed in all sports (which is why the majority of top professional pool players are pretty fair athletes); but after that, pool is all a matter of how you use your brain—both sides.

When I was learning pool, or trying to, here's a typical exchange that would take place between someone whose advice I sought and me:

> "Shoot the 5-ball, kid." (The "kid" will give you some idea of how far back I'm going; it presupposes I avoided Tyrannosaurus rex on the way to the poolroom.)
> "Why the 5?" I would ask.
> "Because that's the right shot."

"Fine," I'd say, hope rising that I had finally come to the right place. "But *why* is it the right shot?"

"It just is."

And there's no question that many top players operate on the same kind of sixth sense, unable to articulate their decisions even if you stick a gun up their nose. The problem with trying to learn from such players is that you can't apply any given piece of advice to the game in general; you have to wait for the identical table layout, or a very similar situation, to come up again. It's not unlike being taught to play a musical instrument one song at a time instead of being formally taught to play the instrument by learning scales and theory.

None of that for us. In this book, we'll examine the concepts of the three most popular pool games, Straight Pool, Eight-Ball, and Nine-Ball, and hopefully you'll pick up some approaches you can put to work the next time you play.

It's been estimated that to build a computer as efficient as the one between your ears, with microchips standing in for brain cells one-to-one, would require a mainframe the size of Chicago's 110-story Sears Tower. Accordingly, you and I ought to be able to figure out how to tell a bunch of little balls to go to hell.

Let's plan the itinerary for your trip to the winner's circle (and maybe the cashier's window). As great a game as pool is, it's even more fun when you win.

1

Advanced Straight Pool

I'm sorry, but I'll just bet you're hitting the balls too hard.

That's not as insulting as it sounds, because very few players ever do learn the knack of stroking softly, not even some super players. Sense of speed is invariably what cuts the trotters from the pacers when it comes to pool, clear on up to the game's highest level. And sense of speed really means sense of the *lack* of speed.

Here's one way to look at it: Big-league baseball players use bats that weigh between 36 and 40 ounces, to try and drive a 5-ounce ball into the next county. Your cue weighs about half what a bat does, the balls weigh just about what a baseball does, and you only have to *roll* them—on cloth—a few feet, frequently a few inches. You begin to get my drift.

My reason for making this point first is that in virtually all pool games (excepting Rotation and its variants, in which the cue ball frequently *must* do some traveling), your sense of speed will contribute greatly to your accuracy. And putting the balls in the subway is what the game is all about. Many modern tables have tightly angled pockets that seem to enjoy rejecting balls that do not come straight down the middle. (Had this feature been introduced during any war of consequence, it would have been quite properly labeled an atrocity.)

But the same object ball that stands there wiggling, refusing to take the subway, and spitting in your eye can be coaxed into falling after all. Just be nice to it and hit it softly and you'll see how nice it can be to you. Why? Because the pocket jaws are *parallel* to one another. (Eons ago, when many commercial rooms charged by the rack rather than by the hour, the jaws were angled, which tended to help balls go in, thus games ended quickly and the rooms cadged an extra few dimes or quarters per table, per hour.) Strike the cue ball too hard and the object ball can rebound back and forth between the jaws. Hit the cue ball too soft, and your object ball has a much better chance of reflecting backward—"holeward"—off the first pocket jaw it touches.

There's a second, equally important benefit to be derived from a soft stroke, too: It means you're much more likely to (a) keep your cue level, and (b) therefore hit the ball more smoothly. To use the baseball analogy once more, any player or coach worth his salt would certainly counsel you to go for line drives with a smooth, level swing, rather than to thrash out wildly for the fences. Next time you're in the billiard room where you play, take a look around and see how few players have the butts of their cues down where they should be. The vast majority (unless they've read this too) are sure to be shooting down instead of through the ball. If the room isn't busy, simply see how many little pinholes you can find in the cloth. You seldom find one of these phenomena without the other.

Make that soft, smooth, level stroke your first objective if you want to play good pool. If you play with any frequency, you should notice an improvement almost immediately; and just how softly most pool shots can be accomplished—even your break shots—will delight your eyes and consternate your friends.

(For a more practical concept than the mere word "soft," a good checkpoint is that the pocketed object ball should not touch the very back of the pocket, but rather tumble in off the lip.)

So relax your grip on that cue butt. Try to "think" the action of your stroke into your arm *from the elbow down.* Your wrist should be as limp as you can comfortably make it. And just as tennis players are taught to concentrate on the racket head, you should focus on the tip of your cue, and the tender force it will apply to the cue ball.

How to Break

First, let's make a small mental adjustment: Being required to break the balls in Straight Pool usually means that your opponent will get the first clear shot of the game, right? Well, yes, but you've got the wrong attitude. Consider instead that your breaking the balls is simply going to leave the first *tough* shot of the game. In the first place, that's just what a good break will do (if it leaves any shot at all); secondly, your break will improve if you learn to think of it as an *opportunity*, rather than a hazard.

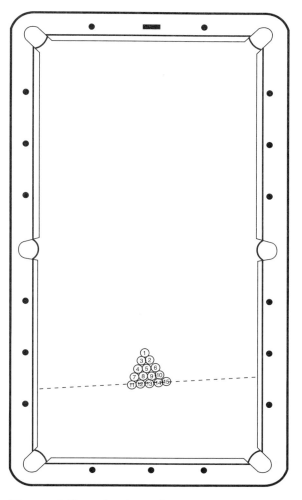

Diagram 1. The rack isn't straight.

Next, I want you to picture the ideal break in your mind: the two corner balls wandering out of the stack timidly, like gophers with an eye out for hawks overhead, and returning back whence they came. This sort of mental rehearsal will benefit every single aspect of your pool game, and we'll be talking about it more. In his excellent book, *Sports Psyching*, Dr. Tutko goes a step further and recommends that whatever your sports event, you should mentally rehearse it *in slow motion* as well as in the speed with which it would normally take place. And if you've taken my advice and slowed down your stroking speed, you're already coming as close as you can, in sports, to simulating slow motion anyway.

Now take a good close look at the racked balls themselves. What we're looking for are assurances that (1) the rack is *straight*, that is, each row of balls facing you is exactly parallel to the bottom rail, and (2) the rack is *tight*, with each ball in contact with the ball(s) next to it. Balls that are crookedly racked, or that exhibit Terry-Thomas-type gaps within the rack, will just about obliterate your chances for breaking the balls safely. (See Diagrams 1 and 2.)

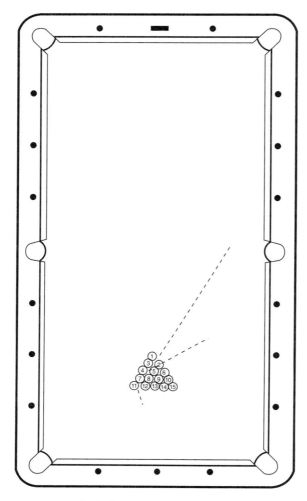

Diagram 2. The balls aren't "frozen."

And the reason you should inspect the rack for these features is not that your opponent is a rascally scalawag with skulduggery in his heart; it's simply that in commercial billiard rooms, or any place where the tables come in for frequent play, it's increasingly difficult to rack the balls precisely. That's because the balls tend to "settle" into thin spots on the cloth, where their last little wiggles will free them from contact with their neighbors. To ensure a tight rack, the player racking the balls should force them together by pressing his fingertips between the wooden or plastic triangle and the balls, by tapping the corner balls with the cue ball, or both.

Now you've got the rack correct on the table, and the break straight in your head. Remember, you're not ready to break correctly without those two priorities.

OK. The break shot is both the first shot of the game and the first shot to which we're going to apply our new theory of minimum force: The *softest* possible hit that will still accomplish the various objectives of any given pool shot is the *best* possible hit.

What we're going to do, accordingly, is take some speed off your stroke and replace it with some spin, or English. Experienced players will tell you to avoid excessive English, and rightly so; but there are several situations when English, judiciously used, can be a very valuable ally. One is when English can help create an angle you need; another is to replace cue-ball speed, therefore to move the ball someplace with greater control, and that's what we're going to do now.

Right-handed players will generally break off the right-hand side of the stack as it faces them, and lefties the opposite, although no rule says you have to. As you learn the fine points of cue-ball control, it may well occur to you that you are somewhat more comfortable in your head with applying right-hand English than with left-hand, or vice versa. (All but the very best players feel that way too, deep down in their heart of hearts; and for some reason, most would rather draw a ball—bring it back toward them—than hit it with follow English.) But let's say that you've chosen to break off the right-hand side.

Set your cue ball along the head string, halfway between the middle of the string (which should be marked with a spot) and the long rail on your right. (See Diagram 3.) Select a point on your cue ball just northeast of its exact middle, but no farther from the middle than the width of your cue tip. (See Diagram 4.) Your point of aim on the

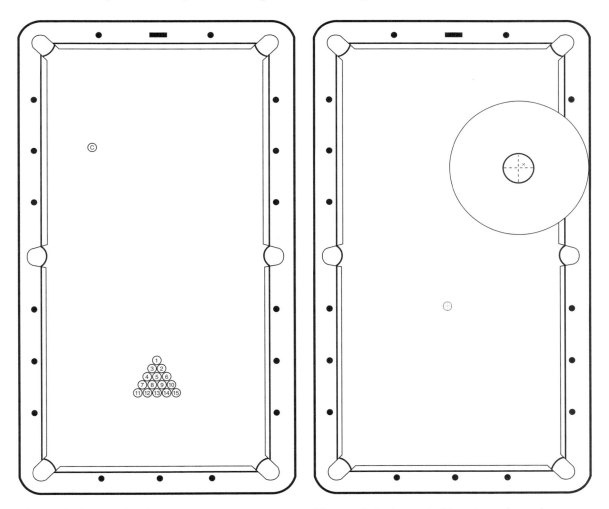

Diagram 3. Opening break position.　　　　**Diagram 4.** Stroke cue ball here (note close-up).

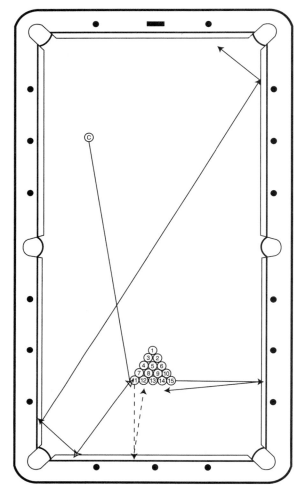

Diagram 5. The ideal break.

corner ball in the rack should be that point at which it is exactly in line with the other four balls in its row (Diagram 5). Now relax and try to *feel* the spin you impart to the cue ball. The correct speed, spin, and hit—and you do need all three—will produce the effect you see in Diagram 5, or very close to it. But on this shot, don't worry about the object balls; you should be focused on the cue ball. The very least you should accomplish is to get the cue ball back to the end rail, or very close to it. That way, if object balls are exposed and pocketable, you've forced your opponent to take the game's first *gamble*, a shot he cannot be sure of and the possibility of breaking more balls open for you. Winning pool is largely a matter of reducing *possibilities* to *certainties*; in competition between two evenly matched players, the winner over the long run will almost surely be the player who gambles the least.

It would be nice if you could break as in Diagram 5 every single time, but it's not the end of the world if you don't. Diagram 6 demonstrates another typical leave which, although playable, still offers positive aspects to you. (Several times over the years I have made *perfect* breaks, in which the two corner balls returned to their original racked positions; and I can't remember a single occurrence in which I didn't lose the rack anyway. You can't always get what you want. As I said, the game imitates life.)

Examining the Stack

Now let's turn the picture around and consider that the balls have been broken by your opponent instead of you, and he has been gen-

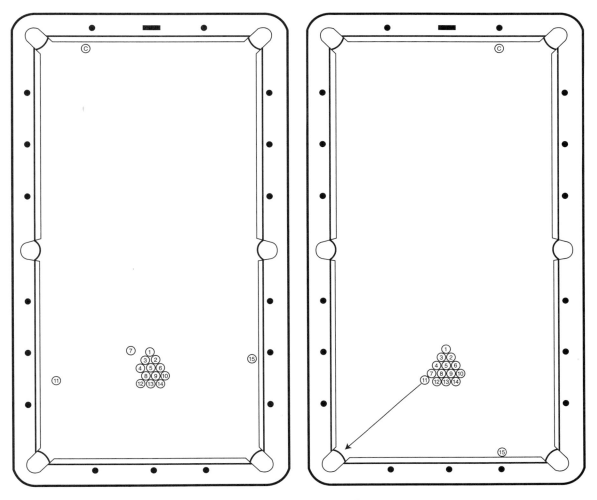

Diagram 6.   **Diagram 7.**

erous enough to leave you pocketable balls. Forget about them for a moment; they only represent possibilities, and we're going to look for certainties first.

You should examine the balls left clustered not only following the opening break, but *every single time that cluster is altered* in the slightest way. It's a very subtle game, remember, and it doesn't take much for a combination shot that can't possibly be made to become one that can't be missed.

Diagram 7 shows you a typical leave off the break that comes up often. Oddly enough, this shot generally occurs when the player breaking the balls has hit his break shot well. You'll note that the corner ball, which is now a mortal cinch for the corner pocket, has actually returned to a position very close to where it began, which would be perfect. See what I mean about subtle differences?

Anyway, his good break has now turned into an even better break for you, and here's how you ought to capitalize on it.

First, remember that in a cluster combination like this, the ball that determines whether your object ball can be pocketed or not is the ball twice removed from it. So no matter how many object balls stand between you and the one you're trying to make, *always read the third ball.* Diagrams 8 and 9 demonstrate a yes-yes and a no-no according to this principle.

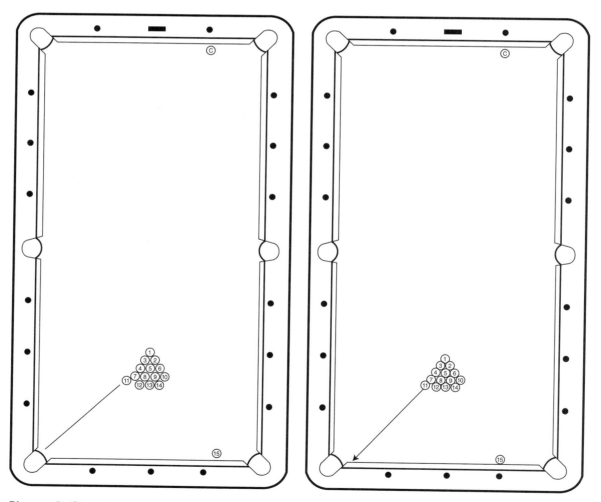

Diagram 8. This can't miss.

Diagram 9. This can't possibly go in.

Let's say that you've read "All Systems Go" for the out-of-the-stack shot you've been left. You cannot help but make that corner ball, and that's a clear mandate to rear back and pulverize that whole rack with one good wallop, right?

I can give you some pretty good reasons not to do that. Play the shot, sure. But play it under control. This is a certainty, remember, and certainties are just what we're looking for; let's not negate our sure thing by introducing the gamble of a howitzer stroke.

In the first place (and we'll talk more about this when we discuss the various single-ball break shots), you'll find that stacked balls react much better to being stroked smoothly than they do to being stroked hard. That's because a smoothly stroked cue ball transmits its force to more of the balls, whereas a cannonball passes its force along primarily to the first ball it touches and the last ball in the row. And as we've noted, it's much easier to achieve smoothness when stroking more softly.

And second, what you're considering is turning your cue ball loose, and that is truly one of pool's epic "Don'ts." The reason could hardly be simpler: When you turn it loose, you don't know where it will end up. So even if you do blast that stack into oblivion, object balls are going to be on all kinds of unpredictable journeys, and they can trap your cue ball, knock it someplace unplayable—or even into a pocket.

What we want to do at all times, in all pool games, is (1) pocket the ball, and (2) keep the cue ball free for the next shot. So even with a juicy cripple such as in Diagram 8, let's not be greedy. Increase your speed from soft to medium, but above all, hit it *smoothly*—and concentrate on drawing it back out of there, toward the center of the table. This will not only do a better job of opening the balls, but it will afford you the maximum options among the balls that are opened.

Let's consider another combination-shot leave off the break. This one looks like a real doozy, but actually it shows up quite a bit. You start looking for this one when your opponent has taken both the corner ball and the ball immediately next to it out of the back row with his break. Now check Diagram 10. Believe it or not, that 9-ball, seemingly buried in swampland, is really a pretty good candidate.

Diagram 11 shows you what you're looking for. The reason the 9 is such a delicious stiff is that it's in immediate contact ("frozen") with the ball next to it, and will therefore be thrown into a can't-miss carom

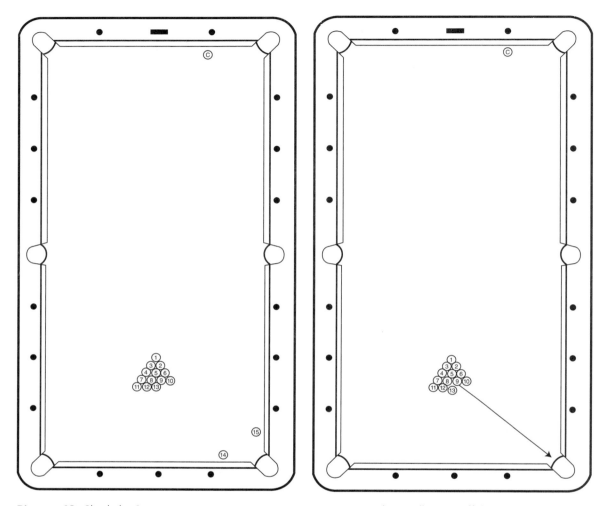

Diagram 10. Check the 9.

Diagram 11. The 9 will carom off the 13-ball in the end row, into the pocket.

off that middle ball in the end row. Remember, it must be frozen on its neighbor, *and* clear of the ball in back of it, or else it's no stiff.

In fact, if the reverse of that situation existed, as in Diagram 12—where the 9 is *not* frozen on its neighbor, but *is* frozen on that last-row middle ball—the 9 wouldn't be within a foot of the pocket. But don't kiss off this situation completely, because with the 9-ball and the ball behind it frozen, the last-row ball—the 13—becomes a pretty good candidate itself, as a carom off the 9-ball. (Incidentally, in carom shots of this nature, it becomes unnecessary to read the third ball removed, as we did in Diagram 7.)

To make the 9-ball in Diagram 10, you need to strike the 3-ball head-on—but because of the position of the 9, you're going to need some speed this time. Just focus on controlling your cue ball; hit it hard and just below the center. We've already determined that the object balls will take care of themselves. Get that white rock back in the center of the table.

The opportunities offered in Diagram 12 are a little trickier to come by. That middle ball, the 13, can only be made by striking the remaining corner ball; again, you'll need speed, and the angle on that corner ball is such that you can't hit it full, at the risk of scratching off

it in the corner. And that means you'll have to turn your cue ball loose, something we want to do as seldom as we can.

So hit the shot with a little reverse (in this case, left-hand) English. That will help negate your cue ball's speed coming off the bottom rail.

I'll limit the discussion of specific out-of-the-pack shots to these, because they do come up with some frequency, and because I obviously can't show them all. (Personally, I find new ones almost as often as I play, but I might never look at that same shot again.) Don't be intimidated by the profusion of words required to explain all this. These are all mental calculations that you'll quickly learn to do in seconds, once you're at the table with the balls, not diagrams, before you—and once you've learned what to look for. The important thing to remember is, always check the stack any time it's been changed at all. Check it from all sides; dead shots are often available to the side pockets and back pockets too.

The legendary, late Willie Mosconi has been quoted as saying, "There's *always*

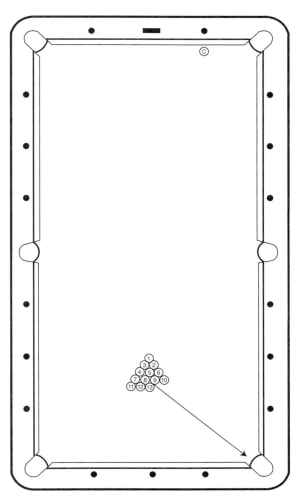

Diagram 12. Here, the 13-ball is frozen on the 9 and will carom off it toward the corner.

a playable ball." (But I wouldn't recommend that you test his theory for the sheer joy of experimentation in any games of consequence. If a shot looks merely comatose rather than truly dead, and you just can't work up your enthusiasm for it, pass it up and look for another option. We're coming to that.)

Break Shots

One way to define Straight Pool itself is to consider it as the only pool game requiring transitions from one rack to the next.

Accordingly, your ability at the game will always be equal to your ability to make those transitions: breaking the balls, and positioning yourself for future break shots. We'll take break shots first, and talk about sequence next, since in the first rack of the game, the incoming shooter following the break will very likely be confronted with a break shot early in his sequence.

Mentally, of course, break shots are among the game's most complex, because your concentration must be equally divided three ways:

1. Pocket the ball.
2. Break up at least some of the other balls.
3. Get the cue ball in the clear.

None of these three is worth a tinker's damn without the rest, obviously. The reason I make such a fundamental point in a book dedicated to advanced play is that a startling number of intermediate and even better players frequently forget about Number 3. They *want* cue-ball liberation, naturally, but they forget to really concentrate on it. And that's just when it doesn't happen.

I agree, splitting up your concentration three ways is no cinch. *Two* ways would be much more comfortable. So why not do yourself a favor and stop dwelling on Number 2 instead?

Here's how I look at it: You already know that your cue ball is going into the clustered balls. It can't miss doing that. You've played position so that's just what *would* happen. There is just no way that you can hit the loose object-ball anywhere near where you plan to and *not* hit the cluster. OK?

Good. Then *close that cluster out of your head and focus on the object ball and cue ball only*. You'll find it just about automatic that if you pocket the ball, with enough speed and smoothness (remember, you *must* have both) to drive the cue ball free of the cluster after contact, object balls will be loose someplace. There is no point in following those balls in flight; you have plenty of time to look at them once they stop anyway. And *the danger in watching the stack is that you tend to jerk your head in midstroke, take your eye off the object ball, or both.* Either mistake is enough to yank you into a half-a-diamond miss.

You've got to "think" that cue ball free, both in your mental rehearsals and your actual stroke.

Once you master that technique, your break-shotmaking will gain immeasurably in consistency, and therefore so should your whole game. You'll find it somewhat harder to do than it is to read about, but stay with it. It'll pay off.

The second major pitfall of break shots, and one that undoes even the very best players now and then, is excessive speed. We've talked about this already, and the principle still applies to break shots as well as open ones: *You can get the job done hitting the ball much more softly than you think.*

I'm not saying you should "baby" your break shots, nor shy away from them. You've got to hit them with authority. But you don't have to clobber them. Just as with those dead combination shots, the temptation is there to drive all the balls apart. But the fact is, you'll play better position, and eventually run lots more balls, if you'll learn that it's simply not necessary to move every ball in a remaining cluster. In fact, it's frequently harmful.

Overhitting a break shot is generally a sign of lack of confidence, rather than the opposite, as you'd expect. It takes real confidence to take speed *away* from the break shot, in my opinion, because of that nagging fear that the cue ball won't free itself. But it will.

Or at least you'll have given it the maximum opportunity to get clear. Again, when you make smoothness rather than power the objective of your stroke, your butt hand is more likely to stay relaxed, your stance will be firmer, and once the object ball is pocketed, you've got the maximum in cue-ball action going for you. There are only a handful of players in the world who can hit a ball with both maximum speed and smoothness, and still maintain their accuracy; and even then, these players are simultaneously sacrificing cue-ball control after impact and putting the maximum number of object balls in flight. That's a perilous combination. You wouldn't *believe* the nasty things that can happen to a cue ball when a break shot is hit too hard.

Which brings us to the third fine point of break shots; again, it's one that escapes even some pretty fair players. *A break shot should be just as precise as you can make it.* The very best break-shotmakers not only pocket the ball, free the cue ball, and get secondary object balls loose, but they have a very good idea of where those balls are going (or at least, the general area of the table). That's because they've looked at their shots carefully enough to know exactly which object ball in the cluster will be struck by the cue ball, at what angle, and the probable consequences.

I know I've already advised you to put the stack out of your mind during the actual stroking of your break shots. But during your mental rehearsal of your break shot (you *are* remembering to do that, right?), which should take place before you even take your stance, I want you to plot the fate of those object balls as though you knew all their birth signs.

And that's not as hard as it sounds. After all, I've already advised you not to put too many of those balls in motion at once; on top of that, remember that you don't have to move a previously unpocketable ball very far to make it pocketable. Millimeters will frequently make all the difference.

Break shots, then, are largely a matter of *control*. Control your emotions about them (after all, they are the game's most important shots); and control your cue-ball speed and action. Control of the broken object balls will invariably follow.

We can't revisit these three points often enough:

1. Focus on the cue ball and object ball *only* during your stroke.
2. Don't murder the shot. It is smoothness that gets the balls open. You'll find that the word *flow* might make a nifty little mantra to chant to yourself as you deliver the stroke; that's just what you want your stroke, and the cue ball, to do.
3. *Know* your break shots as well as you can. No cluster should be a total mystery to you; don't settle for potluck among broken balls, because you can't be sure of being accommodated.

Just as in every other aspect of the game, we're trying to reduce variables to certainties.

Now let's look at some typical break shots themselves.

See the balls specified as 2, 3, 11, and 15 in Diagram 13? Whatever the break shot you're confronted with, those four balls represent the four friendliest neighborhoods for your cue ball to visit. You've probably seen good players place an empty rack on the table while they're clearing the balls off, to determine if certain object balls will be in or out of the rack area; the best players will determine not only if the ball will be playable, but what part of the rack will most likely be contacted—*before* the balls are racked.

The reason those four balls are so desirable is fairly obvious: Each is clear on one side, and that means it will be easier to keep your cue ball free after contact. I'm not saying you cannot break the balls efficiently *unless* you make direct contact with one of the Friendly Four; you can, but you'll generally require more speed, and sacrifice

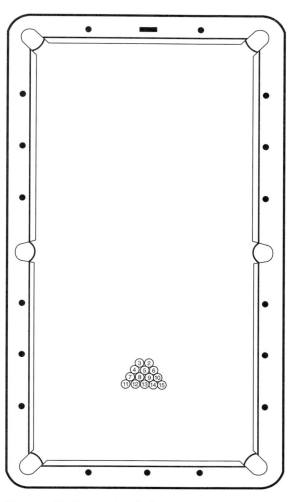

Diagram 13. The best break shots make contact with any of the four corner balls: the 2, 3, 11, or 15.

accordingly in control. The exception to this rule is any break shot in which the cue ball comes off a rail, rather than directly off the object ball, to break up the rack. If your cue ball comes off a rail and *does not* smack a corner ball, it's very likely to stick on the ball it does hit, and you'll have the dickens to pay. (Needless to say, all the break shots you'll see diagrammed here occur on the opposite side of the table too, and are to be played the exact same way. But generally, a right-handed player will prefer break shots on the left-hand side of the table, simply because they're easier to reach, and for the most part that's what we're showing here.)

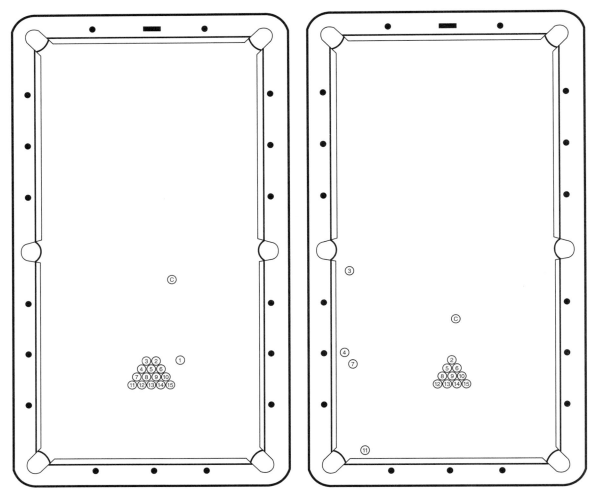

Diagram 14. An ideal break shot, because the cue ball can easily be controlled.

Diagram 15. Typical result of the shot in Diagram 14, correctly executed.

If you could guarantee me the break shot in Diagram 14 every time I had a break shot to shoot, I'd ask very little else of life. Properly struck, this is the very easiest shot from which to get your cue ball to or reasonably near the ideal destination: dead center of the table. All it takes is smooth draw, and no more than medium speed. And it usually moves at least four balls free, in this case, the 3-ball, the 11-ball, and the two balls in between. The perfect speed for this shot will get the 3-ball in the vicinity of the side, the 11 down near the corner, and the other balls in some proximity to one another for another break shot proposition (Diagram 15). But again, concentrate during your stroke on cue ball and object ball only. No two breaks will ever be exactly the same; as long as your Kojak has some breathing room, you should have something to shoot at next.

Diagram 16 looks like the same shot—until you remember to look for the point of contact on the rack, like we just agreed to do. (But you knew that, didn't you? You're coming along fine.) Now you can see that this *is* a different shot than the last, and it's important that you not underestimate the difference.

In order to pocket the ball here, your cue ball is going to have to take on those interior balls between the 2- and 15-balls. And in their way, gram for gram, they can be as fearsome as the defensive Front Four of any Super Bowl team. They've got most of the mass of the rack behind them, and they can stand a pretty stiff jolt without coughing up any turf. So you'll need more speed, combined with the same smoothness, to get your cue ball out of there, and don't be surprised if it heads for the side rail. Hopefully, you'll have the 3-ball available next; most of the other broken balls will have been moved to the other side of the table, which could be a problem if something isn't pocketable on your side.

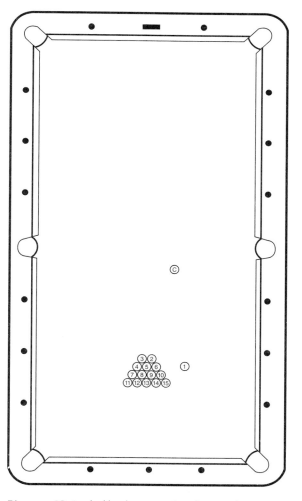

But again, this break shot is nothing to fear; it's just that you ought to know its pitfalls. The shot is mostly a matter of confidence. If you hit your cue ball with anything less than a good firm stroke here, there's a big fat scratch waiting for you in the corner, so bear down and stroke through the ball. You can count on moving close to half the stack with the shot.

Diagram 17 shows you a break shot in which contact originates from the front rather than the side. What we want to do here is smack the 3-ball cleanly, rather

Diagram 16. Looks like the same shot—but it isn't.

than hit in the crotch between the 2 and 3, which would have a vastly different effect on the cue ball. (It might even spit it back in the direction of the side pocket.)

Correctly hit, this shot will demolish the right side of the stack. But you can't draw your cue ball this time, because the force of your stroke plus the spin you pick up after contact would undoubtedly send you way the hell back up the table for a treacherous long shot next, probably off the rail too. None of that for us. We want to hit the cue ball absolutely dead center here. If you make solid contact with that head ball, and stroke smoothly, your cue ball should travel toward the right-hand side rail, *slowly.* If it shows faster sidespin than forward roll, congratulations; you hit it just right. Contact with the rail will cause it to spin back toward the center of the table. The only peril here, again, is overhitting the shot, in which case you run the risk of picking up some natural following English you didn't want, and Baldy will head for the corner rather than the side rail. Medium speed will do just fine.

Mosconi himself called the break shot in Diagram 18 the best of all. While nothing qualifies me to take Mosconi on intellectually or any other way when it comes to pool, it's worth noting that his opinion was formed in consideration of *clay* object balls, while the game has long since gone over to plastics. Plastic composition object balls came into prominence shortly before the advent of sharp-angle pockets, in the late '50s, and they're completely dominant today. As to what kind of difference that makes, ask any player who was around in the days of composition balls, and he'll likely tell you that he had to change important aspects of his game around to accommodate plastic balls. Nostalgia might soak

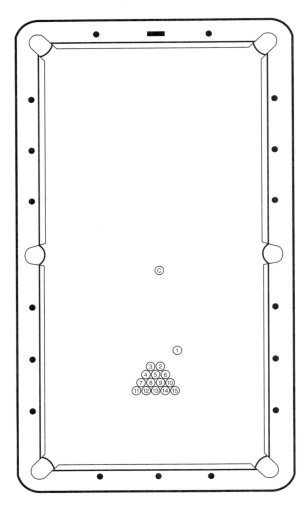

Diagram 17.

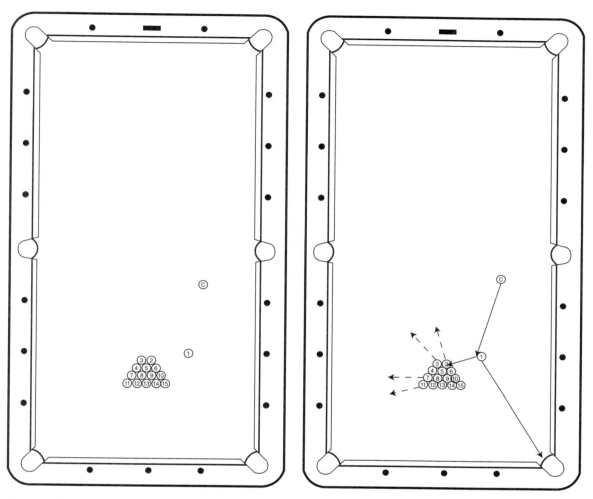

Diagram 18.   **Diagram 19.**

his voice, too; pool with clay balls was really quite a different game than today's game, and lots of veteran players preferred the earlier game. You still hear some grumbling about that, even in the game's top echelons.

So much for technology. What a bang-on hit on the 1-ball, as diagrammed, will do is this: Drive the 1 and 2 smartly out of the rack area; the cue ball will force-follow on through into the *next* row of balls and, hopefully, thence to freedom. (You can't draw this shot, either, for reasons already discussed, and even a center-ball hit on the cue ball will still produce the force-follow effect.) Naturally, you have to hit this shot pretty crisply; but even with smart speed and smooth-

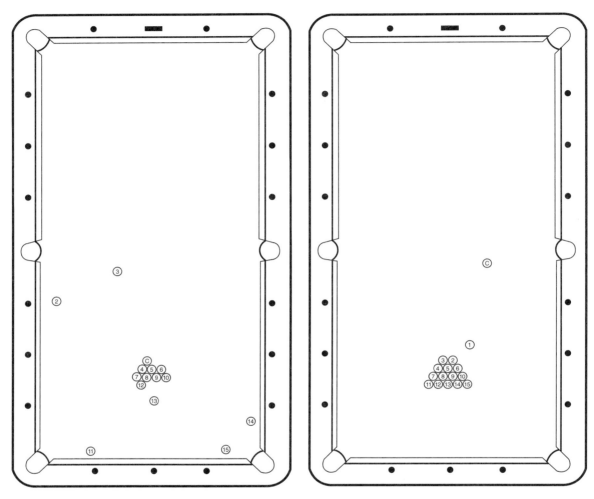

Diagram 20.

Diagram 21. No force needed here; the cue ball will contact the 3 and should come off it toward the side rail.

ness, don't be surprised if you get "buried" in there. It's a bit of hard luck, of course, especially since there will probably be object balls all over that you can't get to. But it's quite a common pitfall of the shot, and it happens to some of the best players in the world. Diagram 19 shows you a typical successful escape route for the cue ball; Diagram 20 shows you the disaster.

I'd rather have the break shot of Diagram 21 than that of Diagram 18, especially considering today's typical equipment. It's a thinner cut shot, as you can see, which means that the object ball absorbs a minimal share of the force you've applied to the cue. This shot, with correct speed and smoothness plus modest follow English—no more than the width of your cue tip above dead center on the cue ball—will move the maximum number of object balls, and may even open the whole stack. The only dues you pay for that are that the cue ball will probably go to the side rail and come back toward the center of the table where all those object balls are moving, and could possibly receive its fare share of abuse, such as winding up frozen on a lone ball. The other demon to watch out for, once more, is excessive speed, which can and often does lead to a scratch in the *opposite side pocket*, believe it or not. I know it will seem like hideous luck if it ever happens to you, but that scratch does exist, and has for quite some time now.

Players seem to settle for the break shot you see in Diagram 22 only as a last ditch; nobody wants to send a break ball into the side pocket. Yet you can turn up old-timers who will swear that the immortal Ralph Greenleaf, surely one of the two finest players ever, chose this particular shot at every opportunity. (Perhaps that's another clue that yesterday's game really was different.)

And at that, you don't have to be Greenleaf to see the merits of this shot. Immediately following impact with the 2-ball, the cue ball will be traveling *forward*—not backward—in the direction of center table, which means you can stroke the shot with less effort than if you were drawing the ball. Side pockets are the widest target any pool table has to offer you. Your cue ball need only fight its way past two object balls, the 2 and the 3, to get to fresh air. And you keep the broken balls at the business end of the table.

If you hit the 2-ball flush in the diagrammed shot, smoothly enough to follow

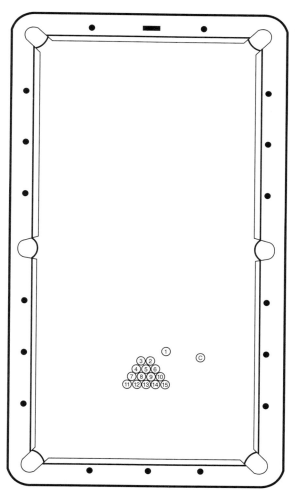

Diagram 22.

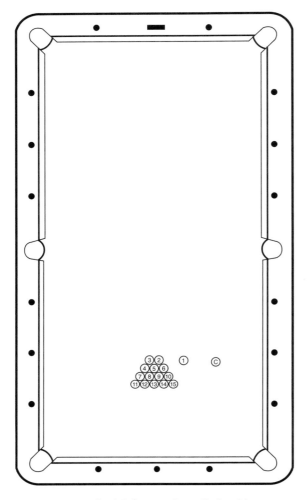

Diagram 23. Nobody's favorite, but still playable.

on through it, the 2 will move in the direction of center table and the 3-ball will travel up near the same side pocket in which you just scored. The 11-ball should move toward the corner, and you will probably loosen at least one other ball at the rear of the stack. (Bear in mind that during any of these shots, you could contact the rack at the ball I suggest but a mere pinhead away from the point of contact I'm talking about, with totally different object-ball results. Once again, I'm simply suggesting what might *typically* happen, along with making suggestions for getting your cue ball free.)

On this and all side-pocket break shots, you simply *must* avoid old Rock-Ribs there, in between the 2- and 15-balls. That is not a worry in the shot of Diagram 22; but if the object ball were closer to the rack, you'd have yourself a sticky wicket. Your cue ball would be forced to attack those middle balls, plus the balls massed behind them, in much the same plane as they already lie, and would have about as much future as Floyd Collins.* You can't hit the shot with draw, either, because you'd be almost certain to scratch in the near corner pocket.

Do your best to avoid side-pocket break shots that require you to cut the object ball thin. Note the difference between the shot in Diagram 23 and the one in Diagram 22. I'd try the Diagram 23 shot if it came up, but I wouldn't like it nearly as much. As a matter of per-

*Mining's most celebrated casualty. Poor Collins was trapped in a Kentucky cave-in the late 1920s. A reporter somehow managed to shimmy down to him and interview him as he lay waiting for his rescuers. The reporter won the Pulitzer Prize; Floyd Collins died while still trapped. Always strive to show your cue ball a kinder fate than that, and the game will reward you in gratitude.

sonal preference, I'd like to be able to see the entire side pocket when lining up a shot like this, and that's not possible in Diagram 23; additionally, although I would engage the front of the rack as I should, I'd have a mountain to move instead of just two balls, because of the angle involved. So I'd have to hit the shot harder, and take potluck with the subsequent position of the object balls. Also, I'd be wary of follow English on this shot, as I wouldn't be particularly eager to send the cue ball on an uncharted flight. Center cue ball would be better here.

Diagram 24 shows you another common break shot in which you must deal with the rack's troublesome balls. It's similar to the shot of Diagram 16, except you're going to follow, rather than draw, the cue ball this time, with enough force to drive through the corner of the racked balls. Your next shot will probably be one of the three balls between the 11 and 15; the dangers of the shot are (a) sticking at the point of contact, and (b) taking too many object balls to the rail with you, which could inhibit if not destroy your next-shot options.

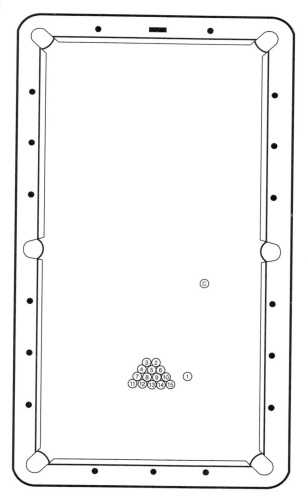

Shots similar to this one may occur where both the break ball and cue ball are fairly close to the racked balls. As a result, you have a shot requiring follow English, yet you really don't have a lot of room in which to follow through on your stroke, for fear of fouling one of the other object balls. When such a shot does come up, you have to shorten (a) your backswing, (b) your stroke, and most importantly, (c) your bridge (in other words, move your bridge hand up on the cue). You won't be able to hit the cue ball quite as smoothly as you would with a longer stroke, but the three shortening measures I propose should still enable you to get sufficient juice on the cue ball.

Diagram 24.

Diagram 25 introduces us to break shots from the rear of the rack. As noted earlier, these are fraught with peril. On this and all from-behind break shots, it becomes more crucial than ever to make contact with the outside object balls, and to avoid the three balls between the 11 and 15. The back row of the rack, of course, is the widest, therefore the toughest to open up. In the shot shown, for instance, you could get away with touching the ball next to the 15-ball, but it would alter the path of your cue ball, and you could very well find it moving back toward what's left of the rack, rather than toward center table. Which, to recall a familiar phrase, spells Trouble.

So hit your cue ball northwest of its center, and concentrate on contacting the 15-ball as full as you can. A smooth follow-through will drive the cue ball to the side rail, then toward the center of the table, and the principal object balls affected will be the four corner balls.

Pay special attention to the 13: the middle ball of the back row. You don't want anything to do with that ball in any form of from-the-rear break shots. There is no tougher single point in the entire rack. If you hit the 13-ball on the nose, your cue ball will stick there and will be well on its way to sucking deep swamp water. If you take on both the 13-ball and the ball to either side of it in quick succession, you're an odds-on favorite for a double-kiss scratch in the corner. So if you're going to save a ball for a from-the-rear break shot, make sure that ball sits one side or the other of dead center of the rack.

The shot in Diagram 26 looks like something that Ray Charles could handle eight times out of ten, but then that first apple presented to Adam was without visible danger, too. Actually this shot rep-

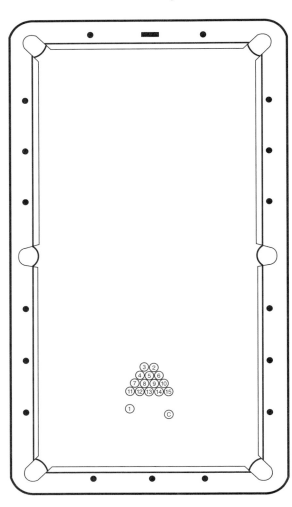

Diagram 25. Note the 13 and stay away from it.

resents a tough little billiard, from the object ball to the 11-ball, which you simply must hit. The farther up the table your cue ball is, at the outset of the shot, the tougher it becomes to take the rack on as you should; ditto as the cue ball is left farther off the side rail. You should hit your cue ball at about five o'clock for this shot. As usual, medium speed will do; and if you engage the corner ball, your cue ball will behave about as it did for the shot in Diagram 25. If you hit the ball next to the corner ball, you can count on either staying between the rack and the bottom rail, or getting stuck on the side of the rack. And if you hit the 13-ball, be prepared to take a seat soon. In any case, don't be deceived by the simplicity of pocketing the object ball; this shot requires the tightest cue-ball control you can muster.

The balls can be broken with the shot in Diagram 27, but it, too, is a shot that players usually choose only as a last resort; it's frequently the result of an improperly played sequence. At any rate, the shot increases in effectiveness with

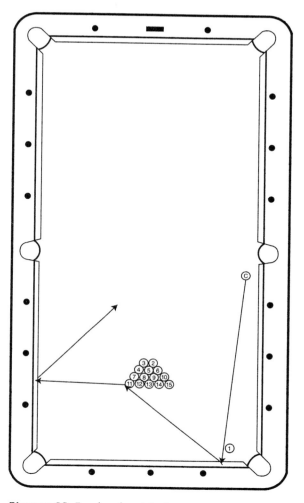

Diagram 26. Tougher than it looks.

the sharpness of the angle between cue-ball, object ball, and pocket. If the cue ball in Diagram 27 were closer to the rail, or the object ball farther from the rail, the shot would be treacherous; you'd have to both overhit it and force the cue ball into the rack, and those are two prime no-no's. As it is, you can pocket the ball with center cue-ball hit or modest follow English; and again, be *sure* you contact the 2-ball on the way back. The inner balls will almost surely capture your cue ball and hold it hostage.

Actually, this is no bargain as break shots go. Even correctly executed, there are still the dangers of a scratch in the opposite side pocket, or a trip to the head of the table, sometimes even a scratch in

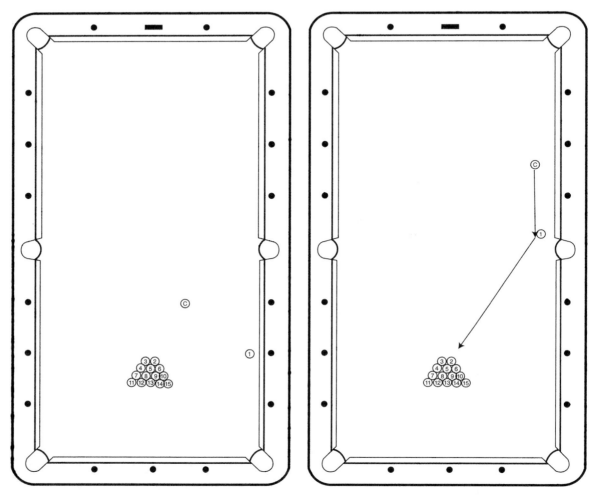

Diagram 27.

Diagram 28. Looks easy—but for best results, you've got to contact the 1-ball position in the stack.

the back corner. The only way to preclude all these horrors is to hit the ball softly; and if you overdo that, you won't do much of a job of opening the racked balls.

As you move the open object ball and cue ball of Diagram 27 farther down the table, toward the corner pocket you're aiming for, it becomes necessary to draw the cue ball, to be sure of smacking the 2-ball on the way back. And that amplifies the chances of sending your cue ball to the far country, up by the head rail.

Diagram 28 presents another deceiver. Pocketing the ball in the side is easy enough, but the shot is completely worthless unless you hit the rack at the 2-ball. If you hit off the side of the rack instead, only Dame Fortune can keep your cue ball out of the subway, and she can be very hard to find. If you overcompensate and hit the 3-ball flush, it's quite possible that the rack won't budge except for the 11-ball, not even if you hit the shot hard; and again, you'll have to get lucky for the 11-ball to wind up anywhere advantageous to you. Once more, what seems like hard luck is really a common pitfall.

If you do hit the 2-ball, though, you'll smash the balls apart. Just be sure you stroke and follow through smoothly enough to get the cue ball off that 2-ball. It can stick there otherwise.

I've left the break shot of Diagram 29 for last in this section because it's the one that seems to confuse intermediate players most. It's neither the shot of Diagram 14, where the cue ball is nearer the middle of the table than is the object ball, nor is it the shot of Diagram 18, where the reverse is true. In the former shot, you draw the cue ball; in the latter shot, you use follow. Now the two balls are precisely in line. How do you hit it?

My opinion is based far more on my observation of top players than on my own playing experience, and it's this: As long as you can make solid contact with the side of the 2-ball, draw your cue ball. At the angle you see here, you could probably even afford to take a little speed off your stroke, and still bring your cue ball out safely while doing an efficient number on the bottom portion of the stack. I know the temptation is there to really rear back and smack this one, especially when things are going well for you and this shot turns up in the middle of a nice run, but don't fall for it. The game can turn fickle on you more quickly than you'd believe, and there's

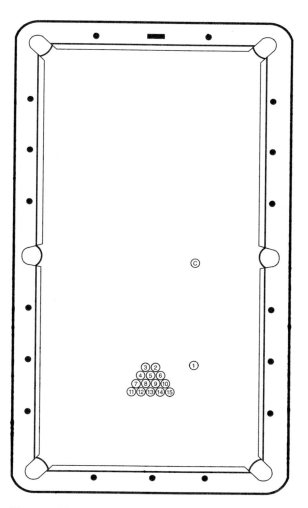

Diagram 29.

no surer way to court disaster than to turn lots of balls loose on uncharted trips.

I don't want to dwell unduly on the matters of stroke and stance; all of the beginners' books on pool have treated those subjects thoroughly and well. But good break-shotmaking is largely a question of good fundamentals, plus the mastery of your attitude about them. The same break shot that terrifies you in the company of those other 14 balls would probably be a piece of cake for you if all of the racked balls weren't there. So you must bring that same nonchalance to the shot, plan it as thoroughly as you can, hit it as though the other balls weren't there, and let your fundamentals take over and do the rest.

The fundamentals I'm talking about include a relaxed rear hand, a fluid delivery and follow-through, and a stance firm enough to restrict your motion to your arm, nothing more. On break shots (in fact, on *any* shots) that require you to cut the ball thin, I think you'll find it helpful to redistribute your weight in the opposite direction of the shot. In other words, a right-handed player cutting a ball sharply to his left should have the lion's share of his weight on his right, or rear, foot, and should lean forward to put extra weight on his left foot when cutting balls thinly to his right. (Reverse all this if you're left-handed, of course.)

Finally, while knowledge is power and all that, and the pointers I am passing along here will complement and may even enhance your accuracy, it's no substitute for that same accuracy. Not this book nor anyone else's is going to sink the object ball for you. I strongly recommend setting aside part of your practice time for getting acquainted with these break shots, and learning what to expect from them. Don't worry about running the balls you've opened up; just set the break shot up, make it, observe the results, then rerack and set up the same shot, or another one. It will cost you a little extra bending and squatting, all that reracking time, but that can't hurt you, and it will pay you generous dividends. You simply cannot play good Straight Pool unless you know how to break the balls; and it's awfully tough to be comfortable with unknown quantities. That's one more respect in which the game of pool imitates life, a point we seem to have made before.

Position Play

Think of pool like this: In order to be champion of the galaxy (this one, anyway) all you really need do is pocket one ball and park your cue ball someplace where you can pocket another each time you shoot. The catch, of course, is that nobody in this or any galaxy can do that every time. But once you've absorbed the pool basics—stance, bridge, aiming, stroke—and develop your shotmaking ability and confidence, the only two areas left for you to improve are cue-ball control and position-play decisions. The former is a matter of how often you're able to practice and compete; the latter can be learned intellectually, by concepts or principles. Since choosing which ball to shoot next is most of the nucleus of advanced play, this will be the most ambitious section of the book.

Before we get to the balls on the table, let's take a slightly more analytical look at the art (and that's what it can be) of playing position in pool.

Experts at the game will generally fall into one of two position-play categories: "tip" players and "speed" players. (A third category of player will pick and choose between the techniques, depending on playing conditions and how things are going.) "Tip" players get their name by using as much of the cue ball as they possibly can, often straying as far as two cue-tips' width to either side of the cue ball's vertical axis. They hit most of their shots at about the same speed (depending upon their cue-ball "juice" of choice), regardless of how far the balls must go. "Speed" players, on the other hand, rarely cue the ball very far from its vertical axis, achieving their position objectives through a combination of center-, high-, or low-ball positions, and whatever shot speed is appropriate. They'll use side English only when they absolutely must (for instance, to alter the cue ball's path to avoid a scratch).

Whichever technique you choose (including the hybrid style), here's a highly worthwhile point: *Your practical outer limit for applying English to the cue ball is the point halfway between the cue ball's exact center and its outer edge.* Get outside that limit, and the risks of miscueing far outweigh whatever additional spin you might impart.

But both position-play methods work, and neither is demonstrably better than the other. Tip players claim speed players can't achieve the same options of cue-ball travel, while the "speedsters" claim that the "tipsters" are making the game more difficult than they need to with the use of all that English. I believe it's largely a matter of what you're comfortable with. I use the "tip" technique myself, primarily because it helps me "feel" the ball better. For what it's worth, the best Straight Pool players—almost unanimously from the East Coast—are mainly speed players. But in Straight Pool, any ball on the table is theoretically fair game for your next shot; Eight-ball and Nine-ball are not nearly that liberal about things, and your reduced next-shot selection may very well require you to spin the cue ball.

It would probably be practical for you to get comfortable with producing that kind of spin, even if you choose to utilize it only when you absolutely must. Staying in the vertical center of the cue ball is almost surely how you were taught the game originally, and adding side English without purpose makes no sense. But all pool games will present you with situations where you simply can't get where you need to go without English to one side or the other. Learning to stroke accurately with side English will require some modifications in your aiming fundamentals; a cue ball struck on the right will deflect slightly to the left of the cue tip, *and* will curve slightly right after deflecting, *and* will throw the object ball it strikes slightly left. (This is equally as true, of course, when you strike the cue ball on the left.) In general, if you're playing a shot using right-hand English, you should aim a tad farther to the right to allow for the cue ball's deflection to the left. Vice versa for left-hand English.

The Right Angle

This is as good a time as any to establish "the 90-degree rule" as a starting point for determining exactly where your cue ball will be going after object-ball contact. When you strike the cue ball in its exact center, the first thing that ball does is *skid* before it picks up its natural forward roll; when it picks up that roll depends on how hard you hit its center. But *if that cue ball is still skidding when it contacts an object ball, it will deflect 90 degrees from the path of that object ball.*

If the cue ball is struck *above* its center, it will roll normally at contact and deflect *less* than 90 degrees. And if the cue ball is struck *below* center, therefore spinning back toward the sender at contact, it will deflect *more* than 90 degrees.

Those last three sentences alone have the potential to make you a vastly better player than you are now. Aiming an object ball into a pocket is probably one of the very first things you were taught; visualizing a second line perpendicular to that object ball/pocket line won't give you any trouble either. And with some good disciplined practice, you can quickly learn to anticipate cue-ball deflections of more or less than 90 degrees, too, depending on just where you need to strike the cue ball. (It's generally believed that sidespin does not affect the 90-degree rule; only high or low cue-ball strikes do. Cue-ball speed affects the angle of deflection exactly as you'd expect it to: more speed widens the angle, less speed narrows it.)

The rule also helps explain why it's so common for one player to leave another nothing when he misses; the object ball hasn't gone where he's planned, ergo, the cue ball hasn't either, and again, pool is a matter of stopping a cue ball someplace. "I wouldn't have been there if I'd made the shot" sounds like a cop-out, and it's as old as the hills, but it's also universally true. Obviously, the 90-degree rule and its variations can't work for you unless you're consistent about getting the object ball into the hole; that's the path from which you're calculating that 90-degree deflection. And, just as obviously, on shots where the cue ball, object ball, and pocket lie in a straight line, there will be *no* cue-ball/object-ball deflection (unless you miss the shot). But most pool shots will have at least some angle to them—and one of the keys to pocketing many balls in a row is to arrange position for yourself, leaving an angled shot each time, because that increases your position-play options many times over. Straight-in shots aren't quite the ally they seem to be (unless they're all you need to win, or lead directly to something else equally simple).

Now let's put these theories to work with some simple applications and proceed from there.

Let's say that the 7-, 8-, and 9-balls you see in Diagram 30 are the last three balls on the table. Regardless of what game you're playing, if you want to run those three balls consecutively, you'll need to sep-

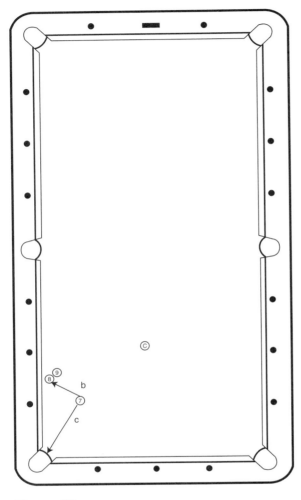

Diagram 30.

arate the 8 and 9 while pocketing the 7. With the 7 lying as you see it, the 90-degree rule tells you that if you hit your cue ball in the center and pocket the 7, the cue ball will travel to break up the 8 and 9.

If the 7-ball were instead at point b in the diagram, you'd want a cue-ball deflection of *less* than 90 degrees off the 7; thus, you'd strike the cue ball above its center.

If the 7-ball were at point c, you'd need a cue-ball deflection of *more* than 90 degrees off the 7, and would therefore strike the cue ball below its center, or draw it.

This is one of the very first principles of pool beyond the sociable stage. All that's required to master it is for you to be aware of it, *and* to hit the cue ball exactly where you aim (the latter can be far trickier than it sounds). Once you begin to understand how to predict your cue ball's travel, you'll be much closer to planning workable shot sequences, instead of just picking off open balls. And what makes the 90-degree rule so valuable is that you use it not only to plan your separation of clustered balls but to avoid open ones.

Understand right now that there is just no reason, in any game of pool, for your cue ball to contact a second object ball that's already pocketable after it hits its primary target. Entire games can turn around instantly based on just that gaffe, even if the second object ball in question is only subtly moved. Some intermediate players assume it's okay to use object balls to stop the flight of the cue ball; it is not. I promise your game will improve by at least 50 percent the instant you embrace this: *Do not allow your cue ball to touch secondary object balls without a purpose.* You will not be able to follow this rule on every single shot—that's part of what makes pool so infinite and fascinating—but you should try to follow this rule on every shot you can.

Diagram 31 differs slightly from the first: Same three balls, any pool game (we can even throw in One-Pocket, assuming the three balls are to be run into the same corner pocket), only this time the 8 and 9 already have open paths to a pocket; thus, it's imperative that the cue ball *not* bother them after taking on the 7. The 90-degree rule tells you that a center cue-ball strike is just what you *don't* want to use here, because if you pocket the 7 while doing so, the cue ball will be headed right for those balls you didn't want to disturb. A cue-ball deflection in excess of 90 degrees is called for here to get correct position on the 8 and 9; thus, you draw your cue ball while sinking the 7—and go right on to win the game. Beginners blunder away opportunities like this virtually as often as they play. Now that you know one simple rule and its extensions, you don't have to.

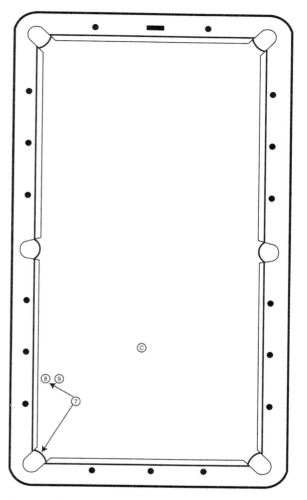

Diagram 31.

The other, and much less subtle, thing you want to avoid doing is scratching the cue ball, and with the 90-degree rule you now have a valuable tool that also lets you foresee that glum fate. The object ball in Diagram 32 is on the foot spot of the table, right where the head ball goes when you rack them all. Its trajectory toward the corner pocket shows you that a center-ball hit on the cue ball would not be very wise here; it would cause your cue ball to head much too close to that side hole. The following three diagrams (Diagrams 33, 34, and 35) show you shots carrying a similar risk. While we can't cover them

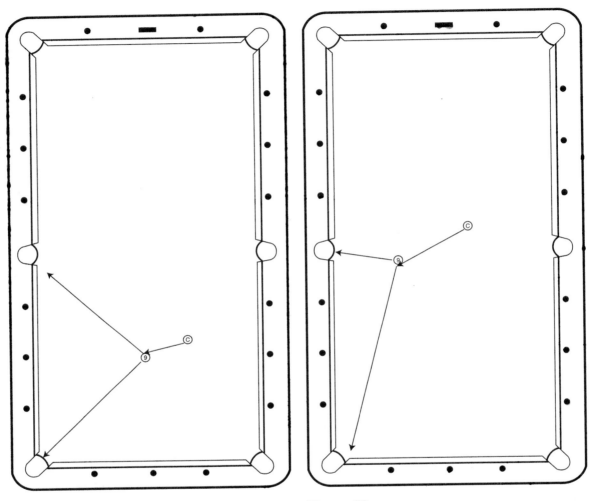

Diagram 32.   **Diagram 33.**

all, we can add this assessment to our individual shot planning at once. Do not take aim on *any* cut shot (namely, any shot where the cue ball, object ball, and pocket form an angle rather than a straight line) without first visualizing your cue ball's deflection from the successfully pocketed ball. You'll need to decide whether that's a path you want it to take and what cue-ball adjustment you're going to make if it's not. Will an above-center or below-center cue-ball hit better serve your position purposes? Why or why not?

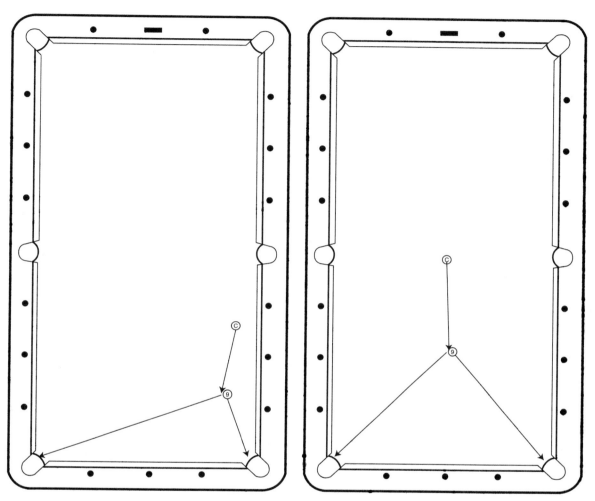

Diagram 34.   **Diagram 35.**

The 90-Degree Rule and Break Shots

The 90-degree rule obviously also applies to break shots where most of the balls are still clustered. Which ball will you be contacting first? At what angle? Can you make an adjustment on the cue ball which will take you into a desirable corner ball instead of a stinky interior one?

Here are a few added rules of thumb that should help you in breaking the balls under control:

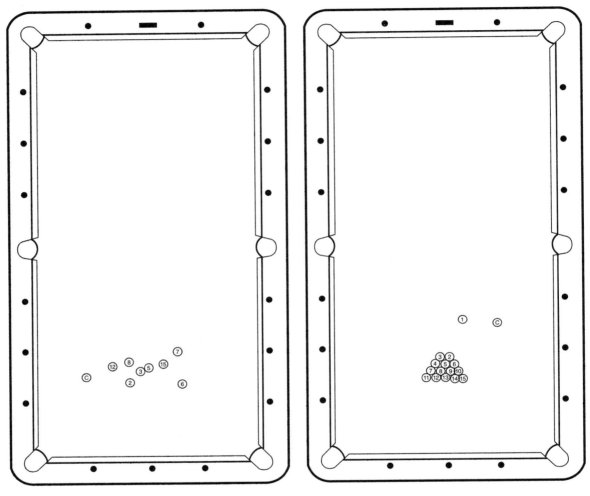

Diagram 36.   **Diagram 37.**

1. Perhaps most important of all, it is *not* sufficient to decide that
   your cue ball will indeed attack the still-clustered balls, and let
   things go at that. You need to determine, as accurately as you
   can, where you'll be contacting that cluster; additionally, you should
   form some opinion as to where at least some of those clustered balls
   are headed. You don't have to chart the flight of each and every one;
   that's a good way to make yourself nuts. But at a minimum, you
   should know which ball in the cluster you'll be striking, and what
   that ball and the cue ball are going to do next. When you break up
   a cluster but still get stuck on an object ball someplace, the majority of the time it will be the ball you first contacted which traps
   you—because you didn't think far enough ahead.

Diagram 36 shows you a typical example of that. The 2-ball is available, but take a closer look at the 3, the first ball you'll be contacting after the 2. There's really nowhere for it to go; it's frozen on the 5 and figures to be trapped between that ball and the cue ball that you've weakened by taking on the 2 first. So there's a very good chance the 3 will trap your cue ball—unless you really blast the shot, which will probably drive most of those balls out of the area when you'd like to keep at least some of them around. Far wiser here to nudge those balls apart by finessing the 2 with sidespin on the cue ball, as discussed in point 5, and save the 6 for the next shot.

2. Experts generally agree that the best secondary break shots, especially those of Straight Pool, are from the side of the rack.

3. A sort of corollary to point 2 is that break shots from behind the rack are overrated. Not only do they carry the risk of leaving your cue ball alone on the bottom rail, but they drive too many balls toward the head of the table.

4. Whenever possible, it's a very good idea to create break shots which allow your cue ball a different path than those of the broken balls. Break shots with which you're able to draw your cue ball already accomplish that, but they're not the only ones that do. Diagrams 37, 38, and 39 show you some common examples, including the correct way to play the otherwise dangerous break shot from the rear. Unless you're absolutely certain that your cue ball will cleanly contact the corner ball in the cluster (from where it can proceed to open space) take this three-rail route with it. A little high-inside English—left-hand in Diagram 39—will help. More about that later.

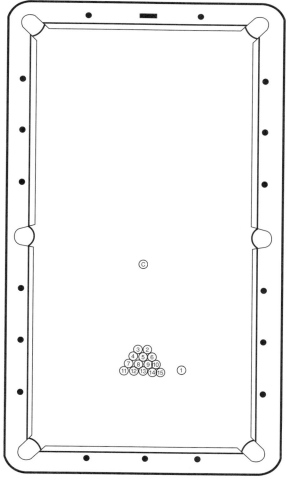

Diagram 38.

On the flip side, if you absolutely *must* send a cue ball into a cluster with follow (therefore traveling in the same direction as many of the broken balls), hit it with a little something extra. You're counting on being able to emerge on the other side by separating all those balls; if you leave a little nucleus of balls, chances are you'll be trapped among them. It's also highly advisable to elevate the butt of your cue *slightly* on such shots; that adds to the cue ball's "force-follow" dynamics.

5. Should you want your cue ball to stay in the immediate vicinity of where you contact the cluster—to avoid traveling toward a scratch, for instance—side English (three o'clock or nine o'clock on the cue ball, depending) will work wonders. The combination of spin and contact with a cluster which outweighs the cue ball considerably will kill its progress dead. Similarly, on shots that are straight-in to a pocket, where you want minimal cue-ball travel after object-ball contact, either hit the cue ball just above center with a little less speed, or just below center with a touch more speed.

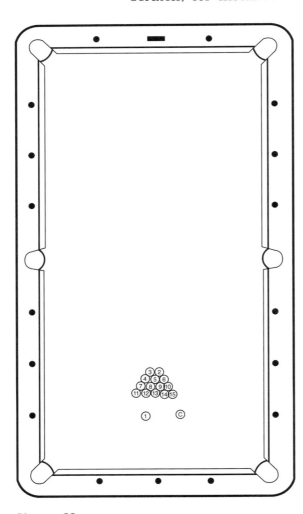

The above tips cover specific situations. So what can we learn about position play in general? After all, any two object balls form a straight line; any three not in a straight line form a triangle. But after that, there's no formal name (or imaginable number) you can apply to the variety of patterns that 14 or fewer balls can form on a 40½-square-foot table.

So how can you learn Straight Pool sequence out of a book, when the possibility exists that you may never encounter the same situations? The answer is that pocket billiards, correctly played,

Diagram 39.

not only presents recurring situations, but that is precisely the objective of the expert player: to reduce those infinite pattern options to that which is familiar and certain. Second, if you're following my advice and controlling, rather than murdering, your break shots, you're driving fewer balls out of the stack, and less far at that. So the possibility of keen similarity, if not actual duplication, certainly does exist, and we're going to talk at some length about how you take advantage of that.

Any game that depends on *improvisation* to the extent that pool does would seem to defy rules of thumb. Still, we'll begin with some generalities, and proceed to examine just how often those generalities apply.

I believe that the underlying concept of Straight Pool is that *whenever possible*—and those are two terribly important words—you should strive to do whatever's easiest.

Now, that in itself represents a gross oversimplification. So let's take a closer look at the statement as it applies to Straight Pool, and what it really means.

1. It means that you don't hit the cue ball hard when you can accomplish the same objectives hitting it soft. Most of what you've already read in these pages speaks to that.
2. It means that you don't apply English to the cue ball when you can accomplish the same thing hitting center ball. English has its place in the game, but you employ it when it's *functional*, not because it's more aesthetically pleasing, or you're more comfortable hitting the ball that way, or (shudder) you took a guess.
3. It means that *whenever possible* (well, I told you they were important words), *you don't move a second object ball that is already pocketable, after sinking the one you called*. It sounds elementary, but just watch the next pool game you see, and take note of how often the players scuttle their own ships by moving balls unnecessarily, even if accidentally. Master the knack of not doing that, and I guarantee you that your game will improve by a conservative guess of 50 percent, likely even more. *Please* learn this.
4. It means that *whenever possible* (w. p.), you don't choose cue-ball routes that require your driving or *forcing* the cue ball, as opposed to rolling it, someplace.

5. It means that w. p., you don't drive the cue ball to a rail when you can get it to an advantageous place without using a rail.

6. It means that w. p., you don't employ two-rail routes where one-rail routes will get the job done.

7. It means that w. p., you don't employ three-rail routes where two-rail (or, sometimes, one-rail) routes will do.

8. It means that w. p., you provide yourself with a second shot that you can count on as part of all your mid-rack break shots. This is the exact same principle as the Safety Valve pass in football. (For those of you who don't follow football, by the way, the Safety Valve is a last-resort, just-in-case proposition in the form of a running back who stays in the backfield on a passing play, so the quarterback can dump the ball off to him if all his intended receivers are covered.) I'm not talking about the specific shots we just discussed, of course, but their smaller brothers and cousins that you use to separate (a good word) smaller-than-fourteen-ball clusters. We'll get back to this.

9. It means that w. p., we position ourselves to shoot at balls on or near the rails early in our sequence. I have to be out-front enough to credit all the pool authors who preceded me for this point, too; it's mentioned in just about all the beginners' books. This time around, I want to give you the *why* behind that tip, and show you where it fits in the scheme of things.

Balls on or near the rails represent two potential sources of trouble: They may block routes that you need to move your cue ball efficiently; and they may also occupy areas into which you may need to drive more object balls on your subsequent break shots. In that case, you only end up creating more miniclusters along the rail, causing you to interrupt the sequence you originally planned and execute more break shots. Remember, the fewer times your cue ball is required to move secondary object balls, the better for you.

Don't worry about remembering all this. Nor will you have to carry my book around the table with you as though it were some kind of pilots' checklist. Take my word for it, experience and confidence will eventually cause all these considerations to come to you spontaneously, and in milliseconds. While you're still learning to put these concepts to work, your play might slow up some; but once you see that these are really the things you need to know, they'll automatically become part of your game.

Now, as to all those "*Whenever Possibles*": What makes the game of pool so intriguing and infinite is the frequency with which it will deny you the chance to take those simplifying steps. You will be forced to violate every single one of w. p.'s, and plenty of times, too. When you are required to do that, your success will depend on how much *control* you can retain over all the variables that confront you at that point. What the very maximum in control will do for you is that it will let you resume your simplifying process at the earliest opportunity. What you never want to do, in this or any pool game, is *guess*. I've said it before: The player who obtains the most certainties for himself is the player who figures to win.

OK. Let's apply these principles to balls on a table, instead of merely on paper. Say that the balls have been broken, by either you or your opponent, and it's your turn to shoot and you do have shots available. Up to now, you've been treating this situation by shooting off the open balls you see, more or less taking potluck about additional shots that might come up along the way, and hopefully some of those will break up the remaining balls for you, too.

Let me see if I can read your mind:

- You can see your next shot or two right from where you are, behind the cue ball.

- You can see there's nothing "dead" in the still-clustered balls.

- You'll compose the rest of your position plan as you go. After all, you came to have fun; open shots are waiting. Let's get at 'em.

There's nothing radically wrong with that thinking; the reason I know it so well is that's what about 98 percent of all players do. It's simply time for you to learn something better, if you're at all committed to improving your game.

The very first step to correct, then, is to *get out from behind that cue ball and walk around the table*. Even if you can identify every open shot from where you stand, take that hike. Use the time to chalk your cue, and while we're at it, use the hand you don't usually use for that. (This will be explained later in the book. Trust me for now—you'll like

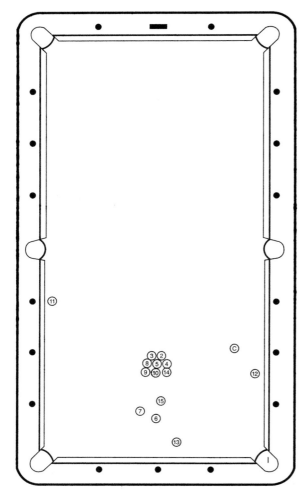

Diagram 40.

this.) You need not make any conscious observations or judgments of the balls' layout; in fact, it's far better if you don't. Just look at that layout from all four sides. Here's why "the hike" will help you play better pool:

1. Ordering yourself to take that hike is one of the early stages of mental discipline, and the latter is something you simply must have if you're to play anywhere near your potential.

2. Your hike around the table will allow you to see which balls go with which as you plan your sequence. Remember the so-called "aptitude tests" you took in grade school? Among them there was probably a category called "Spatial Relationships," which required you to compare and identify similar shapes or patterns. As with anything else, some will be better at this than others.

3. The hike is a pressure-buster. Most of us have to fight off distracting thoughts to focus on the game, and it's the worst when we're in our shooting stance. So get out of that stance, get a little extra confidence, and don't give that negativity the chance to take hold. (Do you need any further convincing that this game is mostly mental?)

4. Your body will appreciate the break from the stance. You breathe a little deeper, because you're standing erect instead of crouched, and it would be a *very* good thing for you to concentrate on that breathing, so that you will be relaxed during your game.

5. Besides all that, your hike lets you see the correct shot sequence, a plan you almost certainly would not have formulated had you stayed behind the cue ball as you usually do. The vast majority of players facing the layout you see in Diagram 40 would try to break up the remaining clustered balls by shooting the 12 into the corner and bringing the cue ball off that side rail. That *might* work— but can you predict what your next shot will be? Not with any certainty. *In all forms of pool, we want to minimize the number of times we take potluck like that.* By all means shoot the 12 into pocket I. But rather than trying it as a break shot, use low-left English instead, and play position for the 11-ball in the opposite corner, getting nearly straight-in. Then follow the 11 to the point where you have a break shot on the 15. (See the opening for the 15 into pocket I? Play it under control and you can be certain that either the 6 or 7 will be your next safety valve shot as long as your cue ball stays in the vicinity. You can accomplish this, by the way, with medium speed and a good amount of nine o'clock, left-hand English, as previously discussed.) You'll have disposed of two balls early—the 12 and 11—which were of absolutely no use to you in this sequence and broken the balls apart, with no risk whatsoever. And just like that, you're playing advanced pool.

That's really what pool improvements are all about: better thinking. Naturally, lots of practice and competition—*especially with players who are better than you*—will improve your shotmaking. But that's something you control, not I. Hopefully, this book will help you get more out of your shotmaking ability.

So definitely take that hike first. Determine your open shots and look for "dead" shots (a ball angled so it can't possibly miss the pocket) in the still-clustered balls. If you don't find any, that means you'll have to use one of the loose balls to break up the rest of the stack later. That's what you'll look for next. And when you're finished doing that, I want you to characterize every single ball on the table, like this:

1. Which balls have open paths to pockets, just as they lie?
2. Which balls *will have* open paths to pockets as a result of your pocketing the A-balls?

3. Which balls simply cannot be pocketed unless you alter their current position? (In other words, which are still unfavorably clustered?)

4. Which of the A-balls or B-balls might you logically use to move the C-balls?

And that's all. Once you've done that, you at least understand the nature of every ball confronting you, and what needs to be done to them. What's left is to decide on the sequence in which you shoot off your A's and B's, in order to move your C's so that *they* become A's and B's. Don't forget, any time *any* secondary balls are moved as another ball is pocketed, your first moves are to inspect the remaining clusters *and* to determine the answers to questions 1, 2, 3, and 4. Try to discipline yourself to go through those two exercises every time you should, without fail. It's perfectly amazing how easily you can forget to do either one under the pressure of a match. All but the best players make that kind of slip.

I promised you real balls on a real table. Let's apply what you've just learned to a modest run of 14 balls. Most of the nine w. p.'s we just considered will arise in even that short a run.

One note of caution: Planning a pool sequence like this takes far longer to read about than it actually does to plan. In fact, you will quickly learn how to plan a pattern like this in a tiny fraction of the time it takes you to read about it here. Don't be intimidated by the amount of words in this explanation.

The idea behind this fourteen-ball run is not that it's any great pool achievement, but rather that it represents the nucleus of correct play. Correct play is actually a very rare thing in pool. All that the very best players really do is successfully apply these concepts of correctness over and over again; thus, their runs go on for racks and racks. Don't worry about how many balls you can run for now (in fact, the more you count your runs, the more likely you are to inhibit them—we'll take a closer look at that later); focus instead on how correctly you run them. The runs that you can ultimately achieve will be dictated by how often you're able to play and your aptitude. Leave everything else to me.

Let's say the break shot shown in Diagram 14—my favorite—yields the layout you see in Diagram 41a. Suppose further that I've already taken my hike around the table and determined that there are no dead shots in the remaining clustered balls.

As you can see, I have six A-balls loose; that is, balls with at least one path open to a logical pocket. That leaves eight balls clustered (C-balls) and the most logical ball to use to open them up (a D-ball) seems to be the 14. Running this rack becomes a matter of playing these balls exactly as I see them now, in this formation, without the need to improvise. In order to ensure that, I'm going to plan a sequence of the easiest shots possible. Naturally, there are specific reasons for shooting each and every shot in the way I suggest, beyond merely sinking one more ball. W. p.'s 1 through 9 form those reasons, and I'll men-

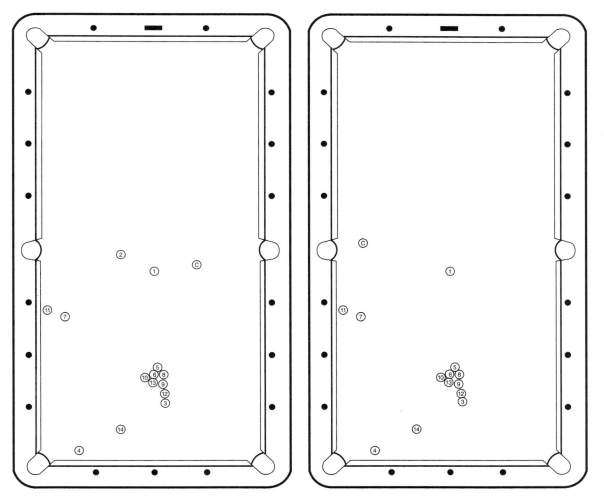

Diagram 41a.   Diagram 41b.

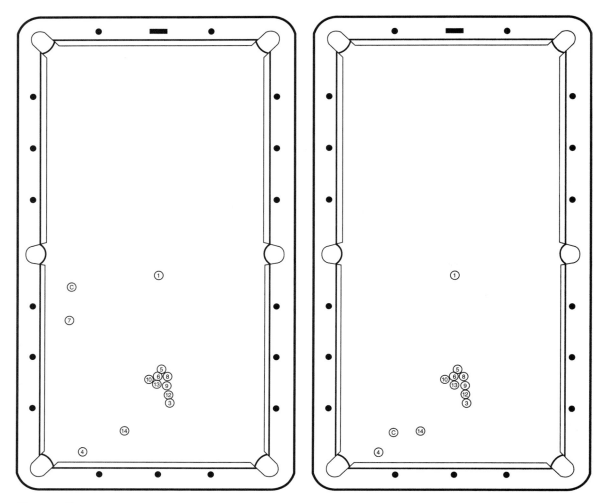

Diagram 41c.   **Diagram 41d.**

tion the various w. p.'s that apply to each shot. (I'll be shooting these at the softest possible speed that still accomplishes what I want to; thus, w. p. 1.)

In Diagram 41b, I've rolled the 2-ball into the side pocket, following up a few inches for position on the 11 (w. p.'s 3 and 5). Additionally, since I don't want my cue ball to be very far off the rail for my shot on the 11, it will pay for me to keep it reasonably close to that rail on the shot before it.

In Diagram 41c, I've taken the 11 off. Using the rail was mandatory here to get the angle I wanted on the 7, but the shot still employs w. p.'s 3 and 9.

In Diagram 41d, I've put the 7 in the subway, a quite simple shot that still accomplishes several objectives. For the first time, I've put w. p. 8 to work. Notice that if I didn't have a good angle on that 14-ball to break the clustered balls, I'd still have another opportunity to get one by playing the 4-ball first. So the 4-ball shot is my safety-valve shot here, and will be on the next shot, too. My next shot will be available no matter what the outcome of the newly broken balls.

So now I'm ready for my second break shot of the rack, the 14. As stated earlier, breaking the balls from the rear like this is not the optimal way to go, but I had no other real choices, and more importantly, I'm not going to drive those clustered balls very far. While I'm easily

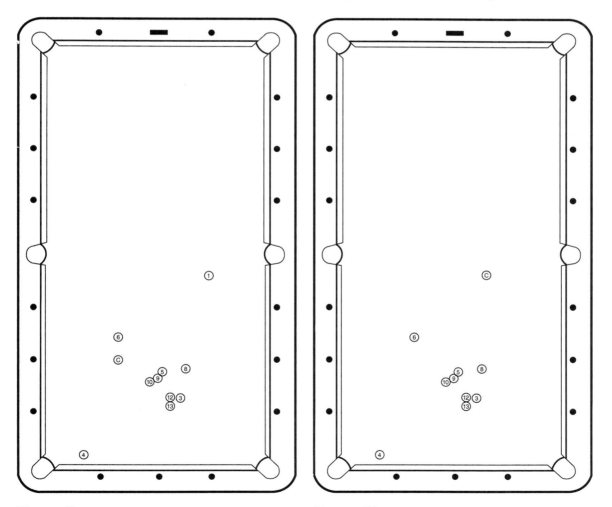

Diagram 41e.   **Diagram 41f.**

capable of a stroke that would pocket the 14 and send my cue ball all the way *through* that stack of balls (and so are you), I'm going to play to drive the cue ball *off* the stack rather than through it. My reason for doing that is that, in pool, probabilities aren't nearly as good as certainties. If I blast that pack to smithereens, I'll *probably* have open shots on the side of the table toward which the cue ball is traveling. But if I reduce my cue-ball speed, I'll *certainly* have the 4-ball to shoot next plus other shots. This proves to be the wisest option and one which allows me to continue playing under control.

As you can see in Diagram 41e, I haven't exactly smashed the pack to hell and gone. But I have hit it hard enough to create some significant and very favorable differences. There are two new A-balls, the 6 and 8, and both are important. The 6 has knocked the 1 over toward the side pocket; the 8 is a D-ball as well as an A-ball, and one that should let me break up the remaining stacked balls with ease. And position on the 8 should follow naturally if I play the 1 straight-in, striving for as little cue-ball movement after contact as possible. I'll check those last six balls for combination shots, but with the layout I have now, I don't particularly need any. (Even though I was saving the 4-ball before, I'm going to take the 1 instead, simply because I'm in such a natural position to do that now. By contrast, I don't have to be anywhere special to shoot the 4.)

Diagram 41f shows me ready to shoot the 8, having made the 1. To be as precise as I can be about this break shot, my cue ball figures to enter the stack between the 9- and 12-balls, and they will break up the rest of the balls for me. So I'll pocket the 9 with follow, with just enough speed to move the 9- and 12-balls no more than a foot or so.

In Diagram 41g, note that I didn't move the 9 or 12 very far, yet all the balls on the table are now A-balls, except for the 12-ball, which is a B. I'd have to shoot either the 4 or 3 to open the 12 up for either corner pocket, but that will be no problem. (While we're on this, opening up paths for shooting balls into the corner pockets nearest where the balls are broken is a critical position move in Straight Pool. Top players estimate that 85 percent to 95 percent of Straight Pool is played at the corners.) Also, note that, although the 5 and 6 appear to be B-balls, too, both are open for the opposite side pocket. The 9 is my break shot for the next rack, and that is something I want to be able to plan as early in a sequence as I can.

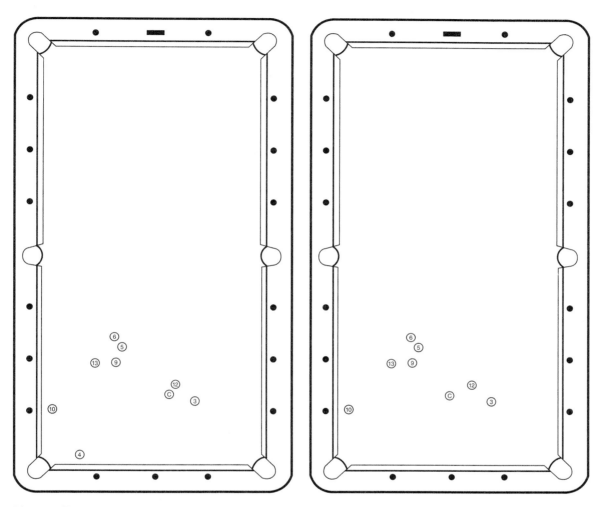

Diagram 41g.　　　　　　　　**Diagram 41h.**

In Diagram 41h, I've taken that easy 4-ball off, and come back off the rail a few inches for another easy shot on the 3. It looks like it would be a cinch to roll my cue ball just past the 12-ball and shoot it next; instead, I'm going to use the side rail for position on the 10. I know that appears to be a violation of w. p. 5, but what I'm really doing is applying w. p. 8 again, and making things easier for myself in the long run, as you'll see in the next shot.

In Diagram 41i, the 3 has been made as described, and the cue ball easily cleared to take on the 10.

Diagram 41j shows you that I've made the 10, and used a little draw on the cue ball to bring it out of that corner area. Now I can make the 13 easily in the back corner pocket. What I want you to see here is

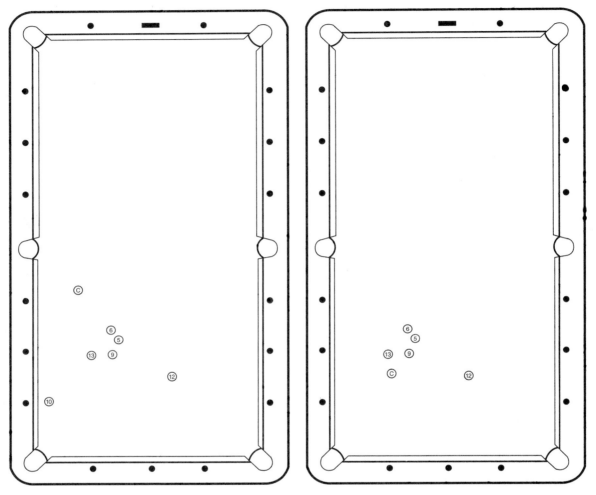

Diagram 41i. **Diagram 41j.**

that if I didn't have quite the shot I wanted on the 13—if, for instance, the cue ball were a few inches closer to the side rail than it is—I'd still have another chance to get good position on the 13 by playing the 12 first. So the 12 has been used as another safety-valve shot and that's why I left it there. As you can see, it's good old w. p. 8 again.

As it is, the cue ball lies ideally for the 13, just a few degrees removed from a straight-in shot. A just-above-center hit on the cue ball with moderate speed will advance my cue ball a few inches, to play either the 5 or 6 next, and Diagram 41k shows you that my next shot will be the 5. I'll draw the cue ball back just enough for a good shot at the 12, as shown in Diagram 41l. Note that, even if my cue ball were a few inches to either side of where it is now, I could obviously still make the 12 and get good position on the 6 with little trouble. Again, I'm not quite straight-in on the 12, so soft draw will move me a few inches toward center table, and a "gimme" on the 6.

And that's just what I have in Diagram 41m. Now I can roll that 6 softly into the side pocket, with a little follow on the cue ball that puts me right where I want to be on the 9. Diagram 41n shows you that's just where I am, ready to break the next rack and start the whole process all over again.

Now, running that rack of balls probably seemed easy compared to the way you customarily struggle in the same situation, so let's ana-

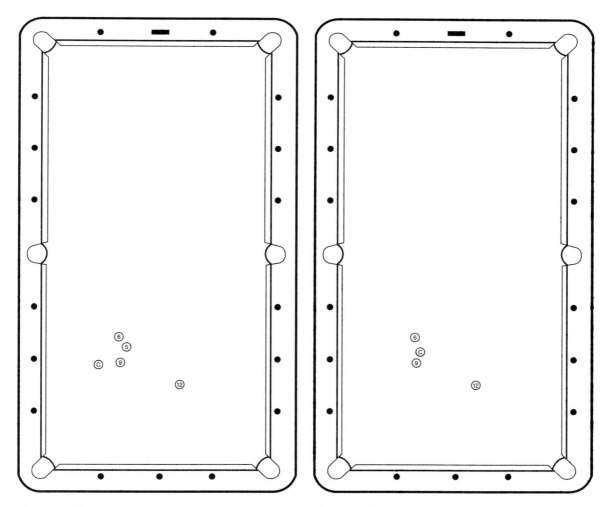

Diagram 41k.   **Diagram 41l.**

lyze why it was such a snap. First, in fourteen shots, I made contact with secondary object balls only three times: my original break shot, the 15-, 14-, and 8-balls. And in each case, that secondary-ball contact was completely by design.

Second, in the fourteen shots, I drove the cue ball to a rail just four times: on the 11-, 4-, 3-, and 10-balls (Diagrams 41c, 41h, 41i, 41j). And in each of the fourteen shots, the distance traveled by the cue ball after contact with an object ball was no more than two feet or so—frequently less.

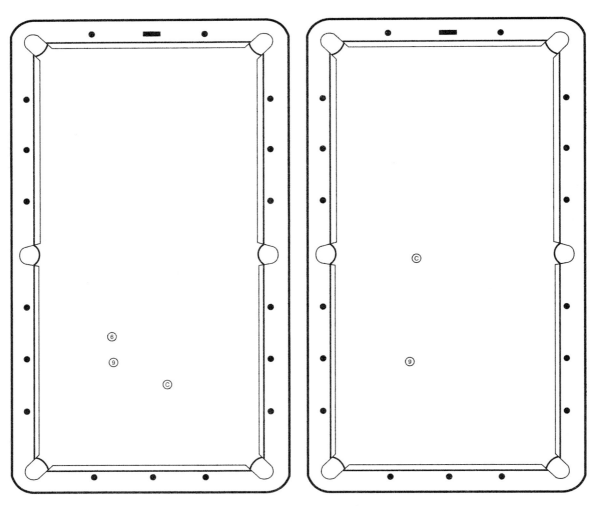

Diagram 41m.   **Diagram 41n.**

I'm not saying I deserve an award for that run. My point is just the opposite: You could have done it, too; if you can run one rack, you can probably run more than one. Analyzed individually, none of those shots was one whit harder than anything you might have come across your first few weeks playing the game. What made the rack so simple was an effective analysis, and that is something you can certainly learn to do efficiently and quickly.

Again, here are your simplifying rules in a nutshell: Separate the layout before you into the categories of A-, B-, and D-balls. (In other words, which balls are pocketable as they lie; which will be pocketable as soon as you pocket one or more of the balls now open; and which you can use to break the unopened balls, or C-balls.) Then it's largely a matter of plotting the easiest possible route among your A's, B's, and D's, much like the connect-the-dots puzzles you did as a kid. No rule says your sequence must take the balls off alphabetically (first your A's, then your B's, then your D's); but as you

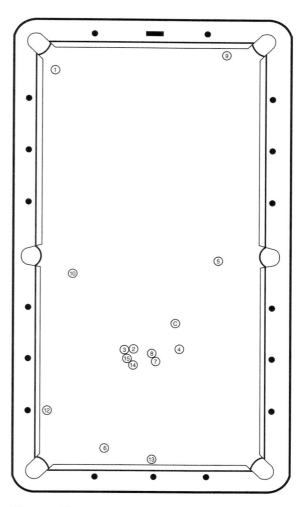

Diagram 42a.

become a more advanced player, you'll recognize that the most effortless racks are those in which you do just that. Just apply w. p.'s 1 through 9 to your mental game, and you'll be putting correct runs together almost before you know it.

Let's examine one more rack situation. In this case, my opponent has broken the rack successfully enough, but dogged his next shot and left me surrounded by object balls. This comes up frequently, even in pool's higher circles, and there's a reason or two for that. In fact, his having left me in the middle of things, as you see in Diagram 42a, is an indication that he chose an incorrect shot that he proceeded to

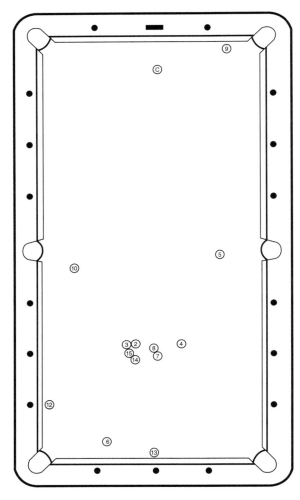

Diagram 42b.

miss. You can tell that without even knowing which ball in the layout he actually missed, and here's why.

With this many object balls loose at once—let's say, more than half the balls on the table, eight in the case of a full rack—you'll generally do better to play your sequence *from the outside in.* By that, I mean to deal with the balls farthest from the original break area first, and close in on the balls still grouped. This accomplishes two things: It lets you save your short-shot, stop-ball opportunities for late in the rack, just when you want them most; and it pays off in better break shots for the next rack, because you're always keeping some balls in the general rack area.

My opponent obviously chose a shot near the rack to begin with, or else he wouldn't have left me where he did. As you can see, there are balls near other pockets, and one of those would have been a smarter shot. Not only would it have allowed him to begin an outside-in sequence, but it probably would have been his easiest option. That's the second point I want you to remember here: Make your first shot following a break shot, or following *any* shot that requires you to take extra aiming time, the easiest one you can possibly find. You want to be certain of continuing your run, of course, but there's a more subtle reason than that. Cinching that first ball is the best way known to man to recapture the rhythm you lost studying that last tough one. And, as you'll read in the following section, you just gotta have rhythm.

OK. Now, the first thing I want to do here is get the cue ball away from that cluster and come back to it after a quick trip up the table for some of those mavericks up yonder. I'll start with the 1-ball (gone in Diagram 42b), a real beginners' delight, but remember, I'm just getting back to the table after sitting a while, and I need to get my rhythm back at the same time I'm scoring. Now my white rock is loose for the other ball down there, the 9-ball (gone in Diagram 42c), and I'm ready to get down to cases.

As you see, I've played position for the 12-ball, a rail shot well worth dispatching early (haven't you been reading your w. p. 9?). In Diagram 42d, the 12 is gone and I'm ready for the 13, for the same reason. Diagram 42e shows me ready for the 6, a simple but critical shot that should position me correctly for the 4-ball, the best D-ball to use to break up the rest. I got where I wanted to be in Diagram 42f; notice also that if my cue ball were a few inches out of line either way, both

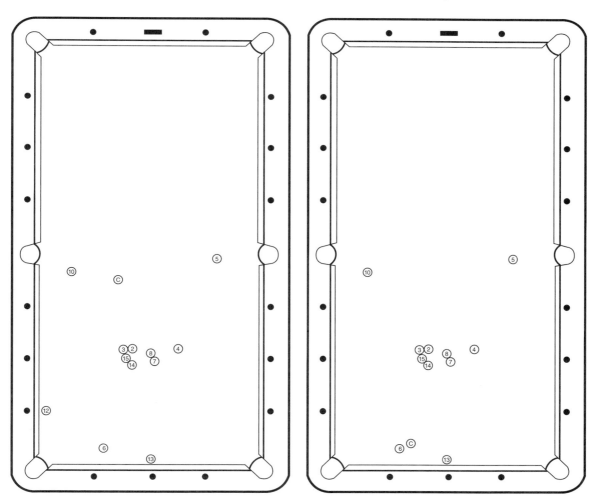

Diagram 42c.   **Diagram 42d.**

the 5 and 10 are excellent safety valves that offer me added chances to get on the 4.

To make the 4-ball as precise a break shot as I can, I note that the 10-ball offers me a certainty following the break shot if I simply get my cue ball free of the 2. So I'll draw the cue ball just hard enough to accomplish that; and no matter where the broken balls go, I'm sure of a starting point from which I can attack them.

But it turns out to be no sweat, in Diagram 42g, all the balls are A's now except for the 8 and 14. They are B's, and will be freed as soon as the 15 and 7 are gone.

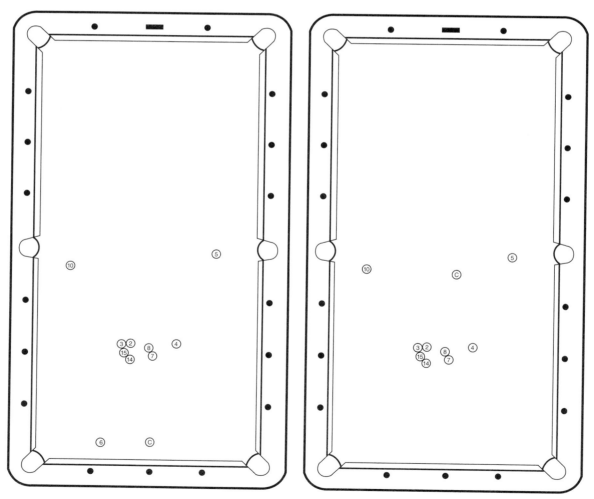

Diagram 42e.   **Diagram 42f.**

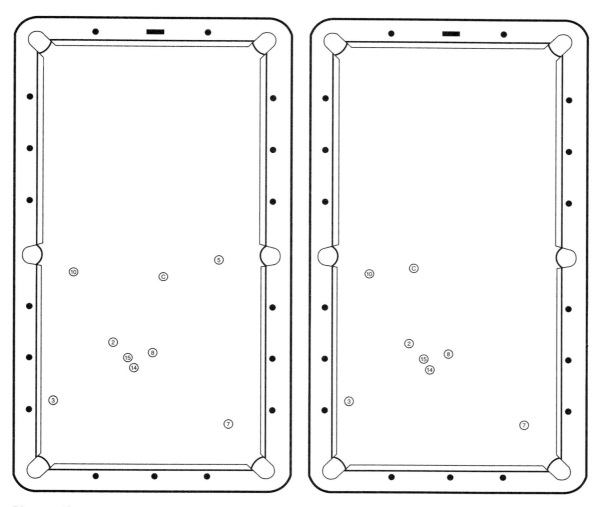

Diagram 42g.   **Diagram 42h.**

It should be candy from here. In Diagram 42h, I've played the 5, and drawn the cue ball back just a few inches for the 3.

In Diagram 42i, the 3 is gone, and I'm on the 7.

In Diagram 42j, the 7 is gone, and I'm on the 15, which is gone in Diagram 42k. They'll all be A-balls from this point on, and you should always note that point at which all remaining object balls become pocketable without further work to do. Diagrams 42k, 42l, and 42m show you that I've bunted in the 8, 14, and 10, respectively, and I'm ready to break the next rack with the 2. (Diagram 42n.)

So except for the very last shot, you can see that the last balls pocketed were those nearest the rack area, a happy circumstance that

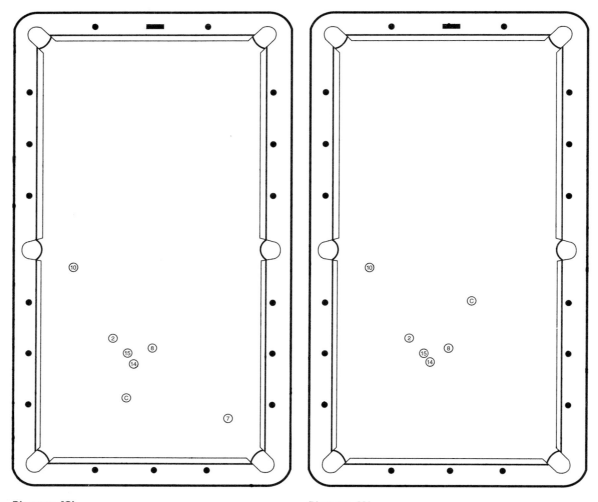

Diagram 42i.   **Diagram 42j.**

almost always provides an excellent break shot for the next rack as
well as a cinch key shot to get to that break shot.

Let's talk a little about a less happy circumstance: What happens
when you *don't* get the cue ball quite where you planned to?

It all depends on how far from your original plan you've left yourself.
If you're stroking softly and smoothly as I've advised all along, and
planning ahead efficiently enough, your failure to stop the cue ball on
a dime should not be all that costly. Diagram 42f is a good example
of how to provide yourself with just those sorts of just-in-case options.

But I don't want to oversimplify this. Pool is a remarkably subtle
game, and I'm well aware that just a few inches, and often fractions

of inches, can turn a game around. I have been both the winner and loser in games in which the turning point had to do with *which part of the pocket a ball was successfully sunk in*; and while that sounds like splitting hairs, it comes up more frequently than you'd expect. That's what makes certainties so desirable in the game.

All right, you didn't get where you anticipated, and now you can't proceed as planned. What do you do?

Well, assuming you've left yourself *something* to shoot at, you should treat this situation just as you would in life: A detour has come up, but you want to return to your original route as soon as it's feasible. Ever since I was a kid and the baseball coaches told me that

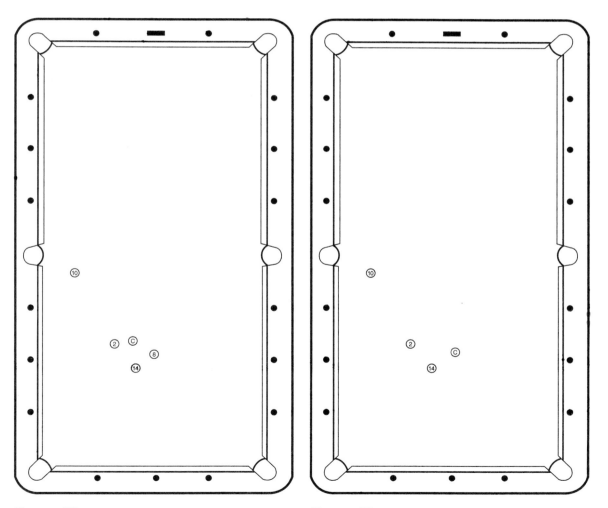

Diagram 42k.   **Diagram 42l.**

baserunners who change their mind about sliding often break their ankles, I've been a great one for sticking with the original plan. In pool, of course, you risk no broken ankles, but indecision can and will put you in your seat, and for many players, that is a far worse fate. So look for an alternate route that can get you back the same way you were going.

If that doesn't appear likely, reevaluate the balls—which are the A's, B's, C's, and D's left to you—and begin another plan, doing your best to stick to that plan. If you've left yourself *no* shots as a result of your miscalculations, don't get mad at yourself; that's all part of the game. Find a safety you can play and shrug it off. Keep in mind that a well-

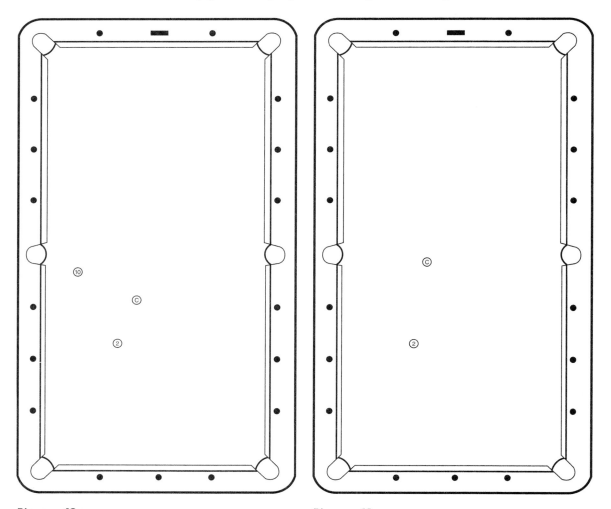

Diagram 42m.   **Diagram 42n.**

played safety will relinquish the table to your opponent for only a single turn. You can wait that long.

Since I obviously can't show you all the factors that might cause you to abandon your plan, or change your mind about it, let's settle for a look at the game's premier mind-changer, in my opinion: the thin cut shot along a rail (Diagram 43). I've seen some very good players (and a whole flock of intermediate ones) go way the hell out of their way to avoid a shot like this in their sequence, even when it was pocketable without disturbing any other balls. The psychology of the shot, of course, is identical to a weekend tennis player's running around his backhand, and a player of any consequence in either game is just going to have to get over that fear. Let me see if I can help.

In the first place, a shot like this, with the object ball frozen or close to frozen, will benefit from correct speed as well as from accuracy. Your lack of confidence in the shot will generally tend to make you overhit it; that is just what

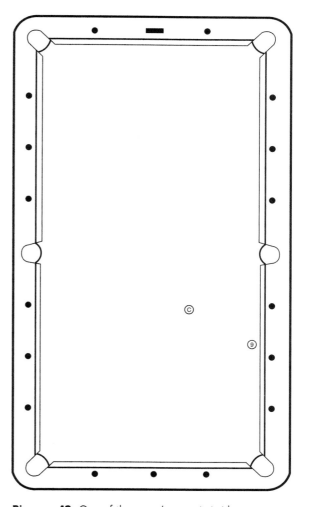

Diagram 43. One of the game's great intimidators.

you should not do. A softer stroke will not only enhance your accuracy but it will let you maximize another advantage: Unless you're playing on new cloth, your table will quite likely have little grooves worn into the felt along the rail. And a softly stroked ball in such a groove is like a plane landing on instruments only, and just as dependable.

The second hint I can pass along for the shot is this: If your shot requires you to cut half the object ball or more, aim at a tad more ball than you normally would and favor reverse English. When you have a fuller ball to shoot at, favor the opposite English—that is, English on the side of the rail in question. These techniques should help change your whole attitude about this sort of shot, and mastering this shot will strengthen your game surprisingly.

At the conclusion of this Straight Pool chapter, I'll give you two layouts to analyze on your own, before reading how I see them (which certainly doesn't mean, by the way, that my way is necessarily the best way; we're just checking to see how well you can extend the principles you've learned).

Remember, none of us will ever live long enough to see all the pool layouts there are. You might say that I've given you the equivalent of an *alphabet* of pool sequence knowledge. Now it's up to you to learn the *language*, and that can take you many, many moons (or it can come to you naturally. It's just like anything else). But you can't learn the language very well without learning an alphabet first.

Before we get to the position problems for you to solve, let's consider some additional position-play concepts.

Tidy Up First

A common dilemma facing intermediate and even advanced players of 14.1 and One-Pocket—games in which the balls are broken open under control—is how to go about separating *all* the balls. (Break shots that separate a fourteen-ball cluster completely are less frequent than you'd think, unless you want to risk overhitting the ball, and it's definitely not worth it.) In either of those games, you will often be presented with a table layout which offers some open shots *and* at least one minicluster yet to be separated. If one of those open shots happens to lie ideally to serve as a secondary break shot, it's all too easy to conclude, "Well, I'm not going to get any better position on it than this—might as well go ahead and break them now."

I can give you reasons *not* to do that: See if you can find a pattern among the loose balls to *restore* you to favorable position for rebreaking the cluster. It's fair to assume you'll be driving at least some of the still-clustered balls some distance on your break shots; open balls you leave lying around now only create more opportunities for miniclusters later. (Also, they clutter your future paths for cue-ball travel.) It's especially important to clear off balls that (a) block paths to corner pockets (close to 90 percent of a Straight Pool game will be played into the pockets nearest where the balls are broken), and (b) lie on rails, which can turn into some nasty miniclusters, besides blocking your cue ball's path. Position patterns from the outside in, which we took a look at earlier, are an example of this.

This rule of thumb carries two important exceptions. One is our good buddy w. p. 8: Whenever possible, leave one ball to serve as your safety valve no matter where your secondary break shot sends your cue ball. (Many expert Straight Pool players believe in leaving one ball on or near the bottom rail until *all* the other balls are open; secondary break shots could send the cue ball in that direction anyway, and if that does happen you'll be grateful for the company of that ball you left.) The second exception is you can leave those open object balls alone for now *if* you're content to nudge the remaining cluster apart gently, rather than blast it to bits. But few players have that kind of patience, and a sensible counterargument is that it might well require running into secondary object balls too many times. (Remember, in all forms of pool, you never want your cue ball to touch a second object ball without a purpose.)

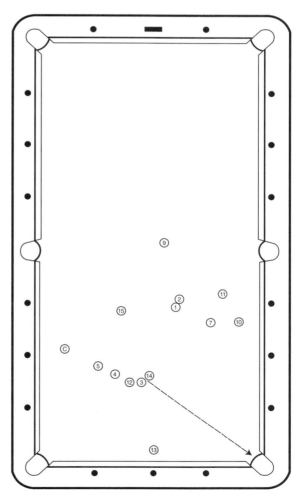

Still, the ploy has its merits, especially if you can see ahead to a key shot-break-shot sequence worth preserving. Let's take a look at both strategies.

In Diagram 44, for instance, the 11-7-10 triangle offers some possibilities for leaving either of the latter two balls as a break shot into the next rack—just the kind of thing that your hike around the table would help you spot. Stay trapped behind your cue ball, however, and you'll probably only see that dead 3-ball straight ahead. After all, that's the last cluster remaining, right? And you're in a

Diagram 44.

position right now where it can't be missed, so let's get to it. Nothing's more fun than a shot you can't miss.

Except that you're not thinking far enough ahead. Do you expect every ball on the table except the dead 3-ball to remain static? Not in this life. Let's count all the reasons *not* to shoot the 3 now:

1. You'll be sending the 14 directly toward that 11-7-10 group we've agreed you don't want to disturb.
2. What can you be sure of shooting at next? If you stop the cue ball near where the 5 is now, the 15 won't go in the corner and lies too tough for the side, and the 1 and 2 cannot be negotiated at all. Additionally, you don't really know where the 5, 4, or 12 are going; and any one of them could visit that bottom rail and maybe even tie up the 13. (One object ball is all you ever want on the bottom rail, in any game.)
3. Even if you draw the cue ball back near its original position for the 15 in the side next, you'll still have moved four balls unnecessarily for the sake of making one; you may well create further problems for yourself to solve.

The solution? Tidy up first and begin with the 15 in the side instead. Ignore the dead shot—what do you need it for?—and use the 4 to gently separate the 12-3-14 cluster. You may even make a better break shot of the 14 than either the 7 or 10 was, as a bonus for playing correctly.

In Diagram 45, it's clear that six balls—the 1, 8, 5, 9, 4, and 12—need their positions altered somehow; none is playable as they lie. The 15 looks like a pretty fair break shot to separate those six; you can get to the 15 naturally by shooting the 2 just before it; and the 11 in the side should get you to the 1 without much trouble.

The thing is, the 2-15 tandem looks good enough for you to save as a key shot-break-shot into the next rack, too. So why not go from the 11 to the 3 instead, and get position on the 14 to nudge those six balls apart? (Secondary break shots from behind like this are generally not recommended with larger clusters; as noted, they drive too many balls up-table and can leave your cue ball deserted on the bottom rail. But here we're talking about taking on just a few object balls, and not moving them far at that. The 7 can serve as your safety-valve shot.)

Like many aspects of life, tidying up first makes all kinds of sense in your pool game. Clear the area for the balls yet to be broken—whenever doing so doesn't require you to go out of your way, or jeopardize your inning. Make it a particular point to clear off balls on or near the side rails, as well as those that open paths to the bottom two corner pockets. It will take a little extra discipline at first, but it provides a focus for your thinking and pays generous dividends almost at once.

Feeling Your Way

A professional bowler once told me, "As soon as the ball leaves my hand, I know exactly what leave I'm gonna get down there [the area where the pins are]."

Now how can that be? The ball contacts the pins nearly 20 yards away; there are several seconds between ball release and pin contact. How can the bowler have any "feel" for a collision between objects when he's physically remote from it?

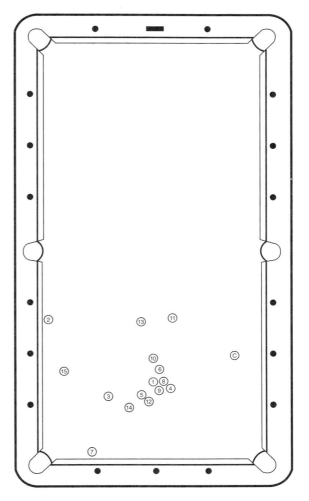

Diagram 45.

Well, he can. "Sixth sense" describes the prescience in hideously clichéd terms; more correctly, the "feel" has to do with that psychological super-sundae of the last decade or so, the right and left halves of the brain. (I'm aware that this prize-winning school of thought has its opponents; I invite your alternative explanations.) Somewhere in between that bowler's aptitude for spatial relationships and his knowledge of his game, he has a picture of which of those finite combinations of pins will be left standing (if any).

Because of his choice of game, he has a few things going for him that you don't: The pins are always grouped in the same general area, and, as noted, there are only so many different leaves possible. In pool, the balls can be legally scattered all over the playing arena, arranged in an infinite number of patterns. Yet you potentially have that exact same ability to "feel" contact between remote objects, and anticipate its results.

If you play Straight Pool or One-Pocket, in which the original stack (and what remains of it after the opening break) is broken with finesse, haven't there been times when you could sense just how the balls would spread? Or exactly what your cue ball would do after separating a minicluster? If you play Nine-Ball or Eight-Ball, don't you sometimes have a feel for when the head ball in the rack is actually going to go in the side pocket on the break? Sure you have—and it was something you just *knew*, without giving any voice to it. That sixth sense (for those of us who have occasionally enjoyed it) is next-to-impossible to describe in words. The point is, it's *imperative* to your game that you learn to bring *feel* into it, in as many ways as you can. Learn to feel the solidness of your stance and bridge. Try to sense the straight-line delivery of your cue to the cue ball. Learn to focus on the feel of your cue against the cue ball; different types of cue joints can and do produce wholly different feels. Whatever it is you've chosen to put on the cue ball in the way of English, try to feel the ball's spin. Every successful pool shot has three distinct sounds to it (cue tip-against-ball, ball-against-ball, ball-in-pocket). Learn to listen for them and for the varying intervals between them according to length of shot.

And by all means, try to develop your sense of cue-ball/object-ball contact. One reasonable way to learn this is to include some dead-stop shots (full-ball hits) in your practice. Since these shots represent pool's answer to running into a brick wall, try to imagine just how *solid* that correct execution will feel. Anticipate your cue ball's coming to a stop without a tremor of spin. Once that sense seems to be in place, apply it to shots that aren't *quite* straight-in, and you'll soon develop a feeling for object-ball cuts as a percentage of full-ball hits. "This will feel about 75 percent as solid as a stop shot" is how you'd describe it, if you were using words.

The important thing is, you don't *want* to use words. You want to *feel* these things, not talk them. Words just get in your way and lead you straight into "analysis paralysis." The most magical thing about the prized "dead stroke" trance is not how many balls you run or how much you win, but just how far from the every-day world of words it takes you. You will probably stop speaking to your opponent(s) or spectators; you may well lose track of how many you've run or when you've made game ball. And all those distractions are rooted in words. Once you succeed in shutting off that word processor between your ears and putting other aspects of your computer to work, you're like a plane flying on instruments—100 percent efficient.

It may not be easy to do without words. After all, a huge fuss was probably made over the very first word you spoke; your life, and indeed all civilization, is based on words. Even lovemaking is rarely completely wordless. And one of the reasons we get into the game of pool as deeply as we do is it's one of the few oases—besides sleep—where we can go to escape the juggernaut, and tyranny, of words.

You needn't metamorphose into an antisocial creep to accomplish this. No doubt the camaraderie where you play is an important factor in your attraction to the game, often as powerful an attraction as the game itself. But can't you wait until the balls are being reracked to do your kibitzing? I can predict with near-certainty that your game will improve perceptibly and immediately the very first time you integrate these kinds of feelings into it. Go try it now!

Inside English—One of the Game's Great Secrets

Let's say you've got a shot requiring you to cut an object ball slightly to the left. Be honest: aren't you often tempted to put just a dab of right-hand English on the cue ball?

This is a more common error among intermediate, and sometimes even advanced, players than you'd think. "But the cue ball is headed that way anyway," the reasoning seems to go, "Why not help it out a little bit?"

There are a number of good answers to this question, starting with "because that makes no sense whatsoever." Here are some of the other good ones:

1. It may or may not make the cue ball curve.

2. It almost certainly will induce some degree of cue-ball deflection (off the cue tip).

3. It will have some effect on the angle of cue-ball/object-ball deflection, because of the "throw" effect. Unless you correctly anticipate that, you'll be missing some seemingly easy shots.

4. It will definitely affect the angle at which the cue ball comes off the first rail it touches. Again, if you don't anticipate that change, you're probably going to be out of position.

You get the idea: These are all potential negatives you're introducing to the simple act of pocketing a ball. Why do that? Even if it seems natural to apply a bit of cue-ball English *opposite* to the direction of your cut shot, don't do it unless there's a purpose to it. Some highly respected instructors teach that there are really only two situations that demand this outside English (sometimes mistakenly called "running English"): (1) To alter the cue ball's path in order to avoid a scratch or running into a second object ball, and (2) when the cue ball needs to be curved to hit a legal object ball. So the very *least* I can do for you in this regard is to encourage you to stay in the vertical center of the cue ball unless you've got a good reason not to.

Except I can do more for you than that. This is a fairly radical departure from conventional wisdom; those who enjoy experimenting with creative problem solving will probably appreciate this more than those who don't. What I'm going to propose is that you consider utilizing the very English you'd normally consider last—specifically, English on the *same* side as the direction of your cut shot, or inside English.

I do have a dated but highly respectable precedent for this: Peers of the late champion Ralph Greenleaf have confided that while the great man was loath to reveal *any* of his secrets, this was one of his best— especially on his break shots. As previously noted, of course, Greenleaf played on considerably different equipment than you and I do: tables with rubber rails, different cloth surfaces, and balls that were made of composition clay or (ugh) ivory rather than plastic—but that doesn't mean the principle should automatically be trashed.

The reason a vast majority of players avoid inside English is because they're unfamiliar with it. It doesn't seem natural to hit the cue ball on the inside; and again, if you can accomplish your position-play objectives by staying in the cue ball's vertical axis, by all means do so. The same caveats about deflection off the cue-tip, cue-ball curve, etc., all still apply. But here are several potential advantages of using inside English:

1. The very least it can do for you is inhibit your cue ball's travel, especially coming off rails. This may be of less value to Nine-Ball players, who frequently must send the cue ball some distance. But remember, in all pool games, especially the precision games like Straight Pool and One-Pocket, each shot boils down to a matter of stopping a cue ball someplace. And this is the type of English that can help you stop the cue ball when it's struck with speed.

2. Similarly, inside English can minimize the angle at which your cue ball deflects off the rail. On balance, shallower-angle cue-ball paths will work to your advantage more often than wider-angle ones; they're more predictable. Let's say, in Diagram 46, you want to pocket the 8,

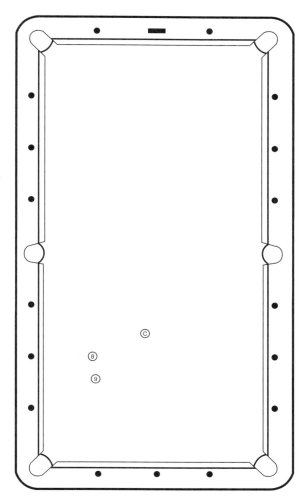

Diagram 46.

send your cue ball to the near side rail, and get an angle on the 9 that will allow you to break up the next rack. That's not hard—in fact, you could accomplish that by hitting the cue ball almost any place you choose—but only inside, or left-hand, English (eight o'clock on the cue ball, for Diagram 46) will let you do that *and* stay reasonably close to the 9 for a shorter, more accurate, break shot.

3. On shots that are not quite straight-in, inside-draw English will help return the cue ball near its point of origin. Neither outside English nor center-draw English can help you achieve anything of the kind.

4. On wide-angle cut shots, inside-draw English can help you achieve wider angles of deflection from the object ball than outside or center-draw English can, should you need those angles.

5. Inside English neutralizes the "cling" factor between cue ball and object ball; thus you're better able to aim the shot as it actually lies.

6. On the other hand, if you want to "throw" the object ball slightly to your advantage, inside English allows you to hit that ball somewhat thinner and thereby alter the cue ball's path accordingly. This can be valuable in avoiding touching any secondary balls with the cue ball, something you never want to do in any form of pool without a purpose. Similarly, reverse English also helps compensate for overcuts.

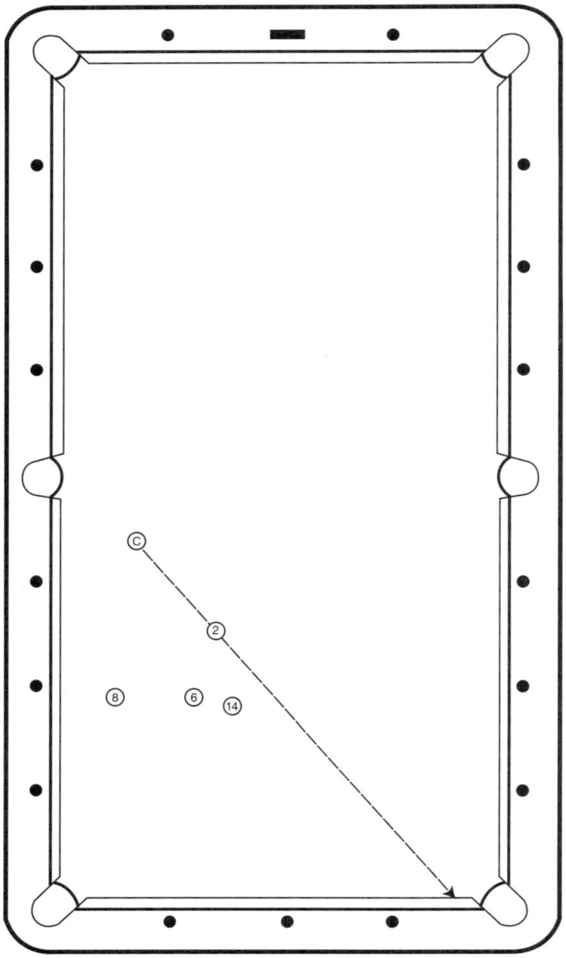

Suppose, in Diagram 47, the game is Eight-Ball and you're shooting solids. If you can pocket the 2 and 6 cleanly, you should have a clear shot at the 8 for game. But your shot on the 2, as it lies, is not quite straight-in and will take your cue ball into the 6 if you play the shot the conventional way, with uncertain if not damaging position thereafter. So, cut the 2 a bit thinner with high left-hand English. That will "throw" the 2 into the pocket while taking your cue ball safely past the 6 and 14, to the bottom rail, and out again for the 6 and 8. (This advice would also apply if the game were Straight Pool, and you wanted to save the 8, 6, or 14 for break shots into the next rack.)

7. If the cue ball and desired object ball are close to one another, inside English can actually help avoid double-hit fouls. That's because you're striking the cue ball opposite to its direction;

Diagram 47.

thus it's on its way by the time you follow through. Outside English, or even center-ball English, can leave your cue tip right in the cue ball's path after contact.

8. Inside English helps you "feel the ball" (that is, become more aware of the sensation of your cue against the cue ball), an absolute must if you're ever to achieve that magical trancelike state called "dead stroke" and scale the heights of your potential. To be fair about things, outside English would do that too, but you wouldn't get all these other advantages.

9. Many players believe inside English transfers a trace of spin to the object ball, especially on shots where that ball lies on a rail or is close to falling in the pocket.

Those are just a few of the playing edges available with this advanced-play tool, and we'll take a practical look at some others. Maybe best of all, it provides a focus for your shot planning. Competitive pressure causes many players, even very good ones, to panic when they're actually confronted with open shots; they can have a very difficult time talking themselves out of all that interference. What inside English can do for you here is force you out of your fog so you can begin concentrating on a concrete, systematized plan: "What's available here that inside English will help me do?" Remember, the experts say that pool is 80 percent mental; if two players of equal ability match up, the one who can conquer his or her mental gremlins and concentrate best will win.

Mental aspects aside, let's consider some very common table layouts where inside English is more of an ally than you think.

One of the most dramatic demonstrations is the Straight-Pool break shot back in Diagram 16 on page 17; this shot comes up all the time. In all such break shots, you know by now that the four corner balls are the optimal areas for your cue ball to make contact, simply because each is clear on one side, which makes it that much easier to get your cue ball in the open. What I want you to notice here is that the object ball lies so as to make that difficult; it's more likely that your cue ball will have to take on those interior balls that lie between the 2 and 4, and those interior balls can be mighty ornery. The best way to convince yourself of the worth of inside English with a shot like this is to set up the shot two times—first, shooting it the way you normally

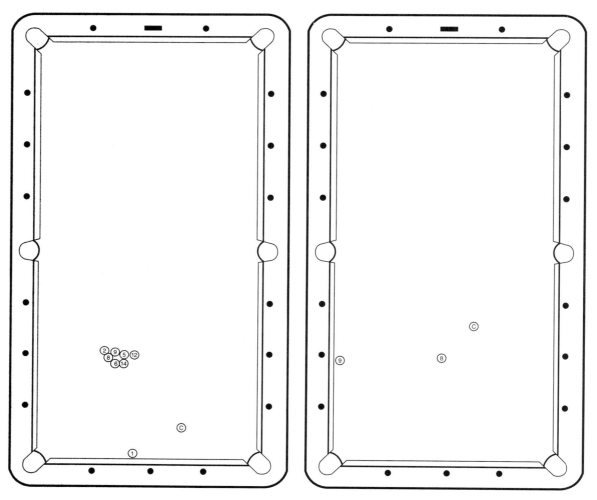

Diagram 48.

Diagram 49.

would; and second, shooting it with left-hand draw, no more than seven o'clock English on the cue ball. I'll wager a few bob that your second try does a better job of separating object balls *and* getting your cue ball free. (Obviously, the shot must accomplish both to be successful.) The reason for that is your inside-draw English is bringing the cue ball back in a straighter line than you're used to (see point 3). Right-hand draw, or center-draw, will take you right into the toughest part of the rack. Left-hand draw will pull you toward the head of the stack, where you belong.

Diagram 48 shows you a consistently valuable and underrated secondary break shot for both Straight Pool and One-Pocket. Rail shots such as these give a lot of novice and intermediate players fits; they are *so* easy to overhit and have your object ball wiggle infuriatingly in the pocket jaws. But inside English—high right-hand, as diagrammed—lets you hit the shot with considerably more speed and less fear. (By the way, the lion's share of pool books on the market have instructed you incorrectly about rail shots. You do *not* want to drive your cue ball where it contacts the rail and object ball at the same time; if you do, your shot won't even be close, because of cue-ball/object-ball friction and the resultant "throw." The correct point of aim is the rail *just in front* of the object ball, a distance about the thickness of a credit card.)

Players will frequently reroute their entire shot sequence, or choose the correct ball but play it incorrectly, simply to avoid having to use inside English. In Diagram 49, if the game is Nine-Ball, many players will choose the two rails to the *left* of the 8-ball as you face the shot, with left-hand cue-ball English, to get position on the 9. The choice braves several risks, none of which is necessary to take: (a) a scratch in the corner pocket opposite where the 8 is sunk, (b) a near-scratch which sees your cue ball flirting with the jaws of that pocket, leaving you in a totally uncertain and rarely useful cue-ball position, or (c) a shot longer than you'd like, and maybe closer to the same rail than you'd like, on the 9. The right execution here is with high-*right* English, and position off one rail rather than two. It solves every problem.

Diagram 50 illustrates how simple it is to screw things up for yourself *without* inside English. If you follow your normal inclination and cut the 8 to the left using right-hand English, you will very likely leave the cue ball close to the rail and the

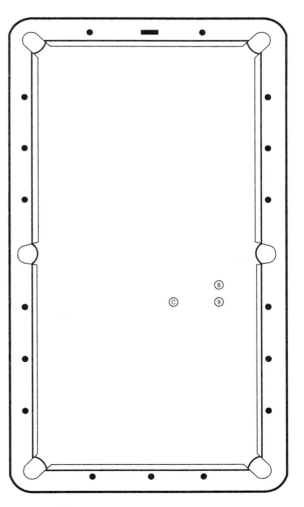

Diagram 50.

9 farther away from it, for uncertain position at best. Inside English (high-left), on the other hand, will send the 9 down the table more closely parallel to the rail, and bring your cue ball farther away from the rail, for optimal position.

Diagram 51 shows you an extremely common situation, in all games of pool. This example is from Straight Pool: Things would be just peachy if only you could draw the cue ball straight back from the object ball—but the object ball isn't straight into the pocket. But reverse-draw—six-thirty to seven o'clock English, as diagrammed—will let you cut the 8 in and still bring you just about back to where you started, for the desired break-shot position on the 9. Center- or right-

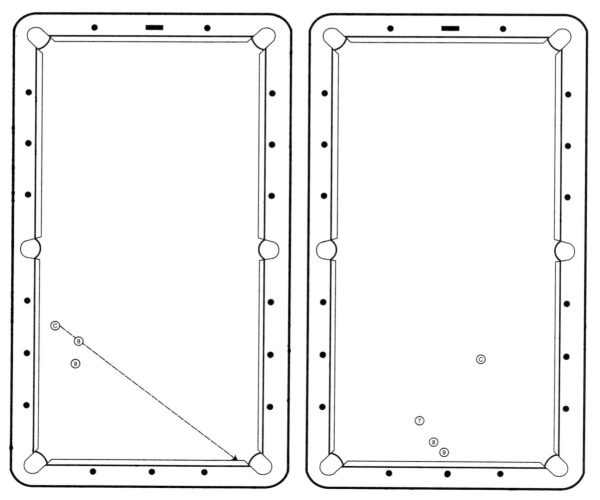

Diagram 51.   **Diagram 52.**

hand draw would bring your cue ball much farther to the right, jeopardizing your break ball.

Diagram 52 demonstrates a pattern we looked at earlier, but your needed angle is more acute here. Suppose the game is either Eight-Ball, Nine-Ball, or One-Pocket, and you've simply *got* to miss the 8 and 9 with the cue ball as you pocket the 7. You guessed it—right-hand draw, somewhere near five o'clock on the cue ball. Anything else will take you way too close to your desired next shots and could rend them unplayable.

Safeties

What do you do when there are no A-balls?

You don't panic and start looking to take a flyer, for one thing. What confronts you now is not necessarily a stymie, but rather a defensive opportunity. And any smart money player, assuming you can get him to talk, will tell you that denying your opponent a shot is at least equally important to scoring yourself.

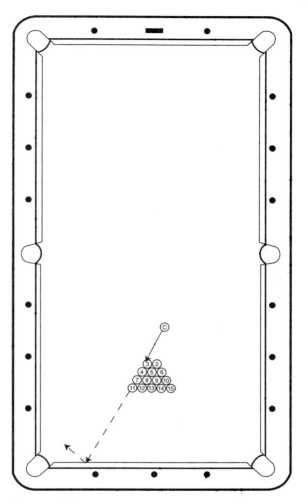

Diagram 53.

An ideal safety, however, will do far more than simply deny your opponent a shot. It will deny him a chance to leave *you* safe as well.

Let's consider closed-rack play first. Suppose the 15th, or open, ball is unplayable as a break shot, or you've made it but still failed to contact the stack.

Diagram 53 shows you a good play from in front of the rack, and what you can expect. Be careful, though, to contact that head ball at a point exactly in line with the balls behind it. If you hit in that crotch between the two head balls, the chances are you will drive no object ball to a rail, and that is not only a scratch but leaves you in deep,

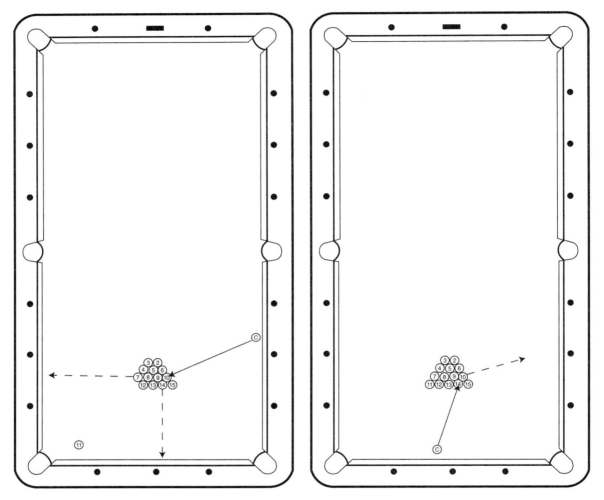

Diagram 54.   **Diagram 55.**

hot water to boot. If you strike the head ball too far to its open side, you'll open that corner ball to the cue ball—just as mortal a wound.

Correctly struck, that safety will leave a corner ball down near its pocket, and the cue ball at the top of the stack.

Since you've now captured one whole side of the table with that open object ball, your opponent will most likely roll out in the direction of the opposite side rail. What you should do here (and it obviously works on an untouched rack, too) is play softly into the 10-ball. Depending upon your angle into the stack, this safety has two points of aim, designated in Diagram 54. As with the last safety, you must strike your target ball in line with the ball behind it (except here you have a choice of two lines). The principal movement will come from the 14 and 7 balls, and both are likely to go to or near a rail no matter where you begin the shot. The speed of the shot is especially critical here; you must stroke with enough force to get the 14, 7, or both to a rail, yet not so hard that they come off the rail and back near the stack. You can see, in Diagram 54, that if the 7 rebounds off the rail far enough, your opponent has a chance to send you up to the end rail with nothing but danger to shoot at. If the 14 comes back near the back row of the stack, he can get down to the bottom rail—not quite as dangerous a trap for you, and you'll see why, but he'd still be out of the trap you were setting for *him*.

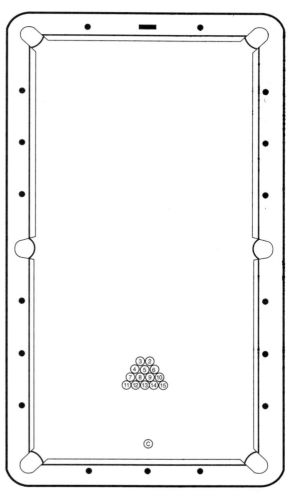

Diagram 55 shows you the same shot in principle, at least, from behind the rack. As long as you can hit the 14 in the line shown, you should be able to drive the 10 to a rail, even if you were frozen on the bottom rail; after all, you're only distributing the force of your stroke out over two balls. This is the easiest safety of the last three to escape, and usually ends up with a shot that challenges either of you to cut it along a rail into a far corner pocket. It's a shot that intermediate players usually want their opponents to shoot first; only the best shotmakers go after it aggressively.

You can do more damage by playing a similar safety off the corner ball, as in Diagram 56. This safety requires that your cue ball be somewhere where you can hit it low—in other words, not on or very close to a rail. You should grip your cue butt slightly tighter for this one, and jab rather than stroke the cue ball; we want to communicate nothing to it but rigor mortis. Aim at a point between the corner ball and about one-third of the ball next to it. Correct kill on the cue ball

Diagram 56.

will leave the mess shown in Diagram 57. I prefer this safety to the one before it because it frequently gets a ball out near the side pocket; makes it quite impractical for my opponent to try anything in that direction; and leaves him a carom, going to his left, that will at least make him think about a possible scratch in the corner if he rolls the cue ball that way.

A move you see frequently among intermediate players occurs when the 15th ball is pocketable but breaking the stack with the shot is impossible. The player therefore announces a safety but pockets the ball, leaving his opponent a full, closed 15-ball rack to shoot at, from as far away a position as he could negotiate. There's nothing really

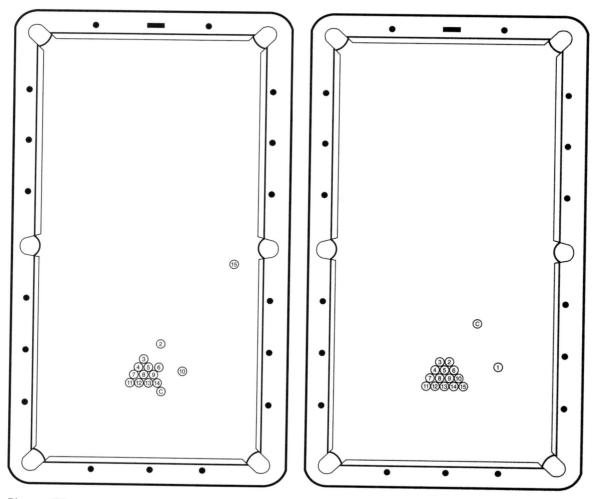

Diagram 57.   **Diagram 58.**

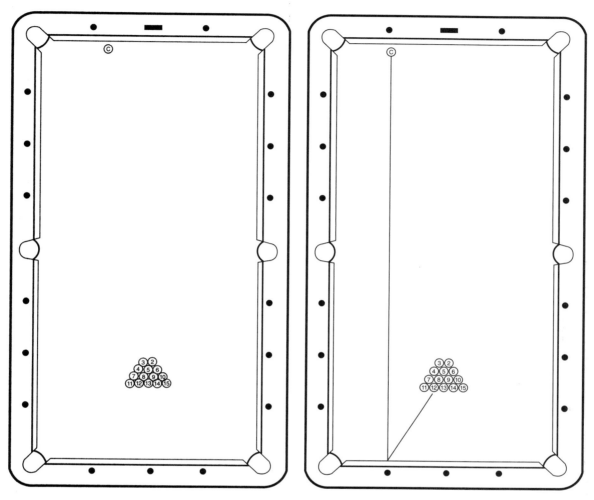

Diagram 59.   **Diagram 60.**

wrong with that move, and it certainly doesn't leave any open shots. But it can be answered, often to the incoming player's advantage. Take a closer look at it.

Diagram 58 shows you a typical situation leading up to this safety: The object ball is straight-in to the corner pocket, and there's no way my opponent can both sink the ball and move his cue ball off the stack. So he pockets the ball and draws his cue ball nicely back near the head rail (Diagram 59). Fine. Except that I have an answer; in fact, a choice of answers. Which one I choose will be a matter of how the game is going, naturally, because the approaches correspond somewhat to the conservative, the median-of-the-road, and the wild-eyed radical.

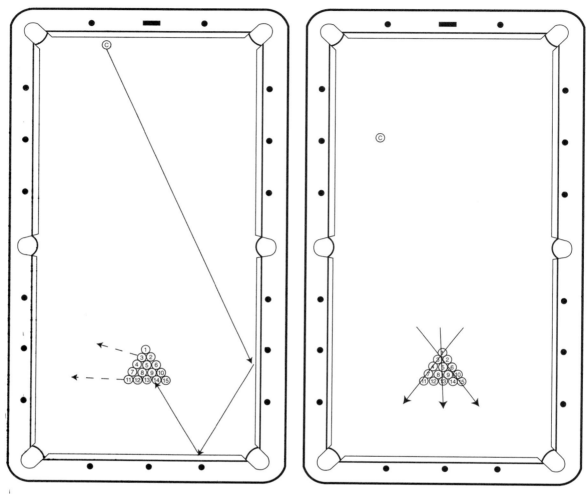

Diagram 61.

Diagram 62. Playable as long as you can make contact with the head ball at an angle equal to any of the dotted lines.

What I won't do—ever—is try to feather either corner ball and get back up the table. It's usually the first thing that occurs to beginners, but forget about it. It's an extremely low-percentage shot, in terms of the probability of leaving nothing open.

My conservative reaction to this leave would be as you see in Diagram 60. I've spun my cue ball off the bottom rail to make contact with the back row of the stack; the 12-ball is the one I want to hit. (You can't spin your cue ball enough to do that, by the way, if you start out frozen to the back rail; make sure the cue ball's center axis is available to your cue tip.) It always looks like a lucky break when you get away with this, but the fact is that you have a pretty good chance to drive the necessary object ball—usually the 2—to the rail, and stick the cue ball in back of the stack. It takes a combination of spin control, speed, and accuracy, but that's quite attainable with practice.

The ultraconservative variation of this occurs when my cue ball is too close to the rail to let me spin it that way. Then I'll do as you see in Diagram 61, rolling *two* rails to come behind the stack and knock out a ball or two. I don't really expect to complete the safety here; it will probably cost me a point, but at least my opponent can't send me back to the head of the table quite so freely now, and I'll probably be able to get the bottom rail in my next turn.

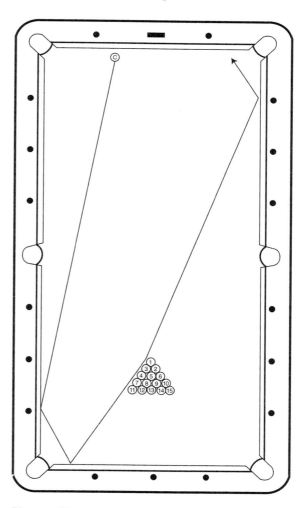

Now for my most likely response, and it's not as hard as it looks. Diagram 62 shows you three points of aim on the head ball, depending upon cue-ball position as shown, center-of-the-table being the most dangerous. I will generally give this a try when my sense of speed is close to its peak, because cue-ball speed is everything here. The same speed sufficient to send either corner ball to the rail (or, from center-table position, maybe both) is the correct speed to stick the cue ball on the head ball. And if, in one of the two angled approaches, you cut the head ball a tad thinner than you really should, you can still get home free; nothing much on that side of the stack should move, and you'll still have that open object ball hidden from the cue ball's view.

There is no sane reason to take on my radical approach to this safety situation, as you can see from Diagram 63. I kind of like the purist challenge to it— perfectly executed, it leaves the stack

Diagram 63.

absolutely unaltered, and as a psych, it's as devastating as a ring of shark fins in your bathtub—but it would take an extremely sociable game to bring the shot out of me.

On the other hand, the great seven-time World Champion Irving Crane would go for this one just about every time it came up, so there you are. (It will probably serve you well to bear in mind that there was only one Irving Crane.) He felt that with his experience, in both reading the correct two-rail angles and cue-ball speed, he should be able to execute this shot acceptably one out of three times; if he couldn't do that, Mr. Crane said, he deserved to take the consecutive three scratches and their penalty (loss of 16 points and being required to break a full 15-ball rack).

The correct speed and spin for this one are elements you can achieve only by playing, not reading. I can tell you that the shot is at its hardest if the cue ball begins near either corner pocket. But spend some time practicing this, using center-ball hits unless you really need to create the angle, and see if you can develop any consistency at it. If you can't, you can't (and few can), but it's a potentially awesome weapon for your arsenal if you can.

You can probably tell, from the choice of responses I have to this safety situation, that my opponent could have done better with the shot confronting him in Diagram 58. What he should have done is pocket the ball as called, *then* announce "Safety" and play the safety of Diagram 54. All he would have had to do is pocket the 15th object ball and stop his cue ball dead, and the shot would have lain perfectly for him, and I'd have had a lot more trouble answering.

The other aspect of safety play occurs, of course, when object balls are already open. If you're playing (and, naturally, thinking) correct pool, your ending up safe in a situation where A-balls exist but are unavailable to you is very likely to be dictated by luck, your bad or your opponent's good. The principles of advanced pool all have to do with minimizing the factor of luck, but the chances are you will never see a pool game that precludes luck completely. Even a game in which a player runs out in his first inning is likely to offer that player some lucky rolls to keep his run going. So make your mind up that luck is very definitely part of the game, and stop cursing fate. If curses could move the cue ball, I would have been a world champion ages ago, along with about ten million other players.

The objective of open-table safety play is exactly the same as before: Leave your opponent not just shotless, but answerless. Your best allies for these safeties, logically enough, are just those areas where you *don't* want to be when you're shooting to pocket something, namely, the stack and the rails.

Balls that are still clustered should be your first object of attention when you get left safe in an open table. It's quite possible you will be able to find "bunt" opportunities of the sort we just discussed, even though the clustered balls are no longer regularly shaped. Diagram 64 gives you an idea of what I mean. Just as you learn to examine a stack for possible dead combination shots, you must learn to examine it to see if it offers you natural safety opportunities.

If you can't bury the cue ball in what's left of the stack, though, it's just about mandatory that you get it to or very near a rail someplace; if your opponent is to be left with any shotmaking opportunities at all, the least you can do is make him work to accomplish them. A frequent open-table safety ploy is to select a nearby object ball that is both unpock-

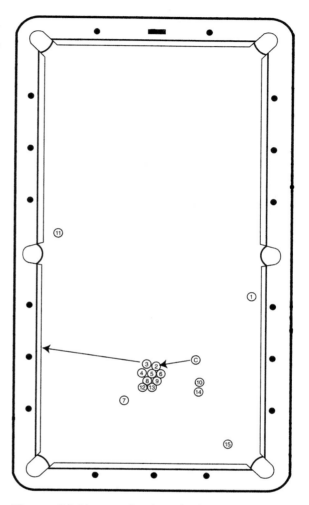

Diagram 64. No open shots here, but by bunting ball 2, I can roll ball 3 to a rail and leave my opponent buried next to ball 2.

etable and near a rail, and duck the cue ball in between that ball and the rail (Diagram 65). This shot is likely to lead to a dreary exchange of bunts unless one of you can get the cue ball frozen to that rail, in which case the incoming player must involve some other rail for a legal safety.

Diagram 66 demonstrates a safety in which you *spoil* a shot that was previously pocketable. Touch is critical here, since the possibility exists that the 1, if hit too softly or too hard, will become merely a second open object ball (or, worse, form a pocketable combination

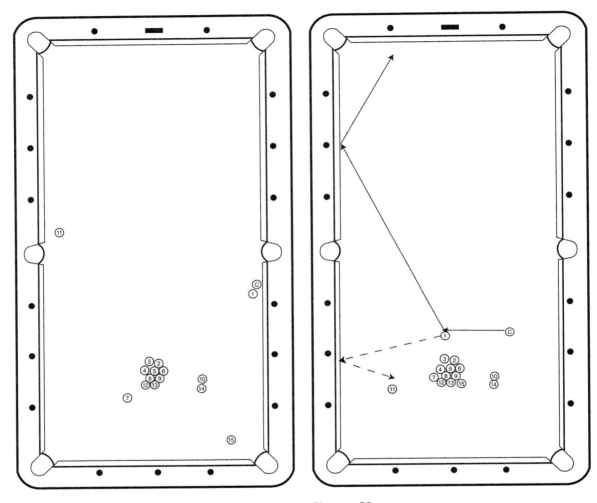

Diagram 65.   **Diagram 66.**

shot with the 11). But this is a shot well worth knowing; you can see how dramatically it can turn the table in your favor when executed correctly.

Diagram 67 shows the same effect—eliminating a previously pocketable ball from consideration—but this time by moving the ball itself. As the shot lies, it's only a low-percentage bank shot or just-about-impossible cut shot; the safety you see in the diagram is far better than either of those, and sends your opponent to the far country without anything to shoot at.

The only acceptable safety plays that leave the cue ball in the center of the table are those that freeze it on another object ball. Diagram

64 shows you that type of situation; you bunt the first object ball to a rail and out of play, and your cue ball limps over a few inches (if that much) to snuggle up uselessly with another object ball. This shot should be made with the shortest, softest stroke that will get the job done; its concept, of course, is quite the same as in closed-rack safeties: minimum force, minimum cue-ball movement.

When no opportunities arise for you to shut your opponent out completely, you're simply going to have to decide what ball, in what pocket, represents the stiffest challenge for your opponent. I've left my opponent a side-pocket shot on the 1-ball in Diagram 68, but I don't think he's going to love it a lot; it's an angle he's not used to looking at, and

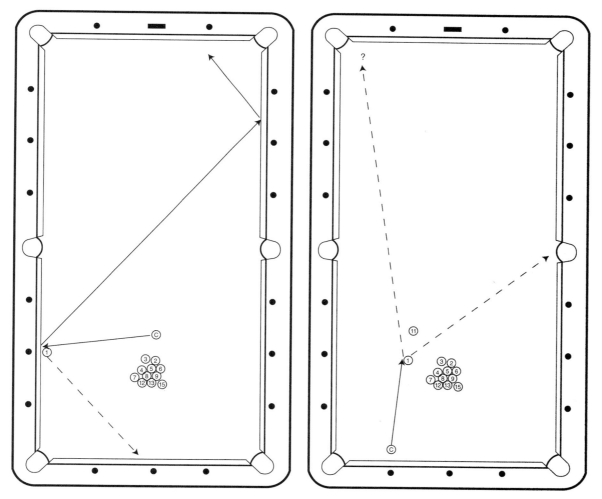

Diagram 67.   **Diagram 68.**

he'll have to turn his cue ball loose for a run up the table, and he must shoot off the rail to boot.

Another safety that will at least make him think is shown in Diagram 69. This is an extremely common Straight-Pool ploy: challenging your opponent to shoot a break shot that figures to either capture or surrender the entire rack for him. This shot depends upon how well you know your opponent's abilities. If you make the open shot too tough, he'll probably duck it; if you don't make it tough enough, he'll hurt you with it. You want to be somewhere in between, as in the diagram, to make it a tough decision for him. The more time he spends pondering that decision, the tougher the shot becomes.

Like good sequence selection, effective safeties are mostly a matter of your ability to read the balls correctly, and think defensively as well as offensively. Both come with practice and confidence. Safety options and opportunities are almost as infinite as pool sequences, but again, I've shown you some common instances that recur, in varying forms, all through the game.

And what you must always—*always*—do before playing a safety is recall whether your opponent scratched in his last turn. If he did, you can get away as easily as by touching the cue ball without moving it, and leaving him your present mess. That costs you a point, needless to say, but it takes the pressure off you and puts it back on him where it belongs. And it brings us to an entirely new area of the game.

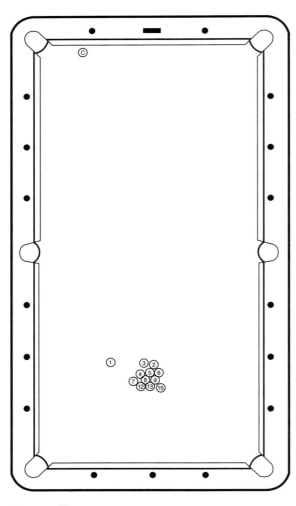

Diagram 69.

Intentional Scratches

It seems self-destructive, but actually this is one of the prize strategies that separate the advanced player from the intermediate one. Diagram 61 showed you one example of such a move.

Intentional scratches are almost entirely a matter of outthinking your opponent, since no balls are going to be moved very much. Their most valuable application, as we just noted, comes up when you're left without a shot and you remember that your opponent scratched in his last turn; the move makes good sense then, and its availability to you adds considerably to the loss-of-point-and-turn penalty he's already suffered for his scratch.

There are times, however, when it makes some sense to incur the first scratch *yourself* with an intentional foul of this type. Suppose my opponent successfully executes the safety of Diagram 54. He has opened up object balls but shut me off from them; worse yet, the only rails available to me, to drive my cue ball toward, will expose those object balls. It's quite likely, in that spot, that I'd do as you see in Diagram 70: nudge the cue ball into those clustered balls. It

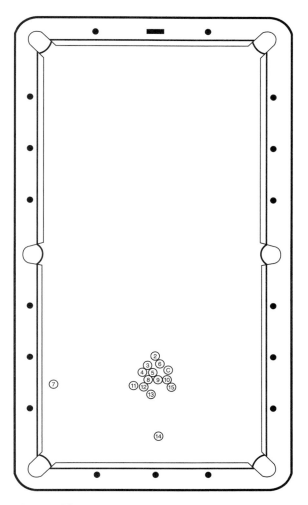

Diagram 70.

costs me a point, but if my opponent falls for this ruse and intentionally scratches back, I now have a chance to play off one of the neighboring object balls to that near side rail for a legal safety, one that hides the open shots and removes my scratch from the records while preserving his. What my opponent should have done, instead of scratching back, was beat me to that legal safety, so I would still have a scratch against me.

The whole trick to intentional safety play is to see what your opponent sees. If your opponent takes an intentional scratch and you have no scratch against you at the time (and remember, three consecutive scratches carries the largest single penalty in the game), you know he's got a legal safety or even a flyer of a shot in mind within his next two turns. So you've really got to think this situation through: What is he going to do to avoid that third scratch? Having determined that, you either beat him to it; alter the balls so the opportunity ceases to exist; or, if there don't seem to be any safeties available to him and you think he's going for a highly improbable shot after all, let him cut his own throat. By now, you can probably see that the art of looking ahead in pool applies to way more than just shot sequences.

If the shoe is on the other foot, and it's *you* who is forced to plan on a low-percentage shot to work your way out of an unsolvable situation, by all means try and lure your opponent into taking two consecutive intentional scratches with you. The advantages of this become clear once you've taken your flyer: If you make it, it's your table with the balls very likely open *and* two scratches on your opponent, which means that you can turn any trap you encounter right over to him with another intentional scratch, and he must respond to it at once. And even if you miss it, you can still get lucky and leave him safe, with those same two scratches staring him in the face; or, you can get semilucky and leave him a tougher shot than he'd like, made considerably tougher by those two scratches and the danger of a third.

So learn to think ahead, both with shots open and when shut off from shots. And never lose sight of your opponent's having scratched in his last turn. Your forgetting that can make a whopping difference in the game.

Rhythm

Eyesight is the first prerequisite of the game of pool. But rhythm comes second, and few players realize how close a second it runs.

I can't think of a game on earth that turns the offense over to you so limitlessly, once it's your turn. In Monopoly, the only way you can get a second consecutive turn is to throw doubles. Even majestic chess offers you only one move at a time. But in pool, you're alone and free as long as you can keep yourself that way. No one is permitted to block or tackle you to hinder your offense (unless you play in unruly places). No one can move the balls to make them harder for you to hit. Freedom is yours as long as you put an object ball in the subway and keep the cue ball free for another shot—in other words, as long as you keep doing the same thing over and over again. And it is highly unlikely, in pool or anywhere else, that you will ever be good at executing repetitive events unless you recognize the rhythm of what you're doing.

Don't take my word for this. What I want you to do is check out what I say, the next time you have an opportunity to see an advanced pool player really hitting his stride. He's running balls, sure, but there's a lot more going on than his merely running up the score; and everything he's doing mechanically can be interpreted in terms of rhythm. Make note of the following checkpoints, apply them to the expert player you're watching, and see if I'm not right:

He spends about the same length of time over each shot (excepting, of course, those points in his sequence where he needs to think or rethink).

He takes the same number of practice strokes, before actual contact with the cue ball, on each shot (except for the toughest ones).

He hits all his open shots at pretty much the same speed.

His actual stroke differs only slightly in speed from the speed of his practice strokes. (The backswing and follow-through of the actual stroke will probably add speed *slightly*.)

His movements between shots will almost always be at the same speed. Some players are faster than others, of course, but I'm talking about an individual player's consistency here. (Conversely, one of the first signs that a player has discovered chinks in his armor is when he visibly begins to slow down between shots.) You'd never guess that physical movements that have nothing to do with the pocketing of the balls themselves could have such an important effect, but they do.

Even so innocuous a movement as the chalking of his cue will be uniform, smooth, and rhythmic, and he'll probably do it while in motion rather than at a standstill. (Cue-chalking, besides preventing miscues, is a valuable aid in establishing rhythm.)

In short, the player you're watching has become *fluid*. Although all the points of sequence we've covered thus far are occurring and being put into play by him, it's very likely that he's not giving them much conscious thought at all; his thought processes and responses have become ingrained and automatic. The term "unconscious" may come to mind, especially to his disgruntled opponent, but that is a wise word indeed. So there he marches, piling his run right up there, rhythmic as you please, higher than herbs could ever get him.

Good for him. What about you?

Well, like most other things, you can't make it happen all at once. Rhythm will occur to you only through practice and confidence. Here are some pointers for you to consider *as* you practice; they will become habitual if you are to be a good pool player. (Which, by the way, does *not* necessarily indicate that you misspent your youth. That statement is alternately attributed to Samuel Butler, Oliver Wendell Holmes, or Mark Twain, and it's a safe bet that any man uttered the quote shortly after being beaten by a younger man.)

The correct situation in which to begin to infuse rhythm into your game is with shots you feel comfortable about making. Eventually, needless to say, you'll feel comfortable with a vast majority of the shots you see; for now, let's consider those shots that correspond to the easy end of your shotmaking spectrum.

Your rhythm should begin even before your practice strokes, in the manner in which you address and assume a stance for your shot. I'm not saying that you have to choreograph your moves in this regard, but you should try to get down the same way as much as you can. If you look around next time you're in a billiard room, I think you'll see intermediate or beginning players who look like they're bobbing for apples while getting into position. Their heads will come up for two or three last-second looks before they're finally down, and I'll bet that they had middling success with the shot in question. Not only did they fail to achieve their rhythm from the outset, but those bobbing heads are a good indicator of indecision, and that's poison.

In watching Mosconi play (and how I wish all of you could have), one of the *added* joys—even after the ungodly shotmaking and position play and other surface things—was the man's remarkable grace. Mosconi was not tall, and was never slender, but you never saw anything as fluid in your life as Willie Mosconi assuming a shooting position. It almost looked like he was parodying himself, it was so perfect, and I know others noticed it too because you could actually hear a giggle or two.

When baseball hitters hit a slump, the first thing their coaches look for is not their swing, but their stance. Stance is just as critical in pool, and for the same reason: It's where your rhythm begins. I'm not going to tell you *how* to stand; all the other pool books do that. I'm just saying that getting into that stance can be a subtle, yet valuable, aid to you. Strive to do it the same way each time, however you do it.

Practice strokes have been covered elsewhere, too; all the experts say no more than three to five, except on shots hard enough to require more, and that certainly needs no verification from me. What I'd like to add is that those practice strokes should approximate the speed of the stroke you're planning (and have mentally rehearsed, right?). It is not imperative that your practice strokes match your stroke speed *exactly*; I think you'd find that difficult to achieve anyway, because of your added backswing and follow-through. But I don't want you to stand there idly sawing wood just because you were told to; these provide a dress rehearsal for your stroke, and deserve that kind of attention. The habit will pay you back well.

So concentrate, until you no longer need to, on taking the same number of practice strokes, at least on your shots of average-or-greater ease, and make them a clocking of the speed for your stroke. Watch good players, too, the best you can find; you'll see testimony to the effectiveness of this.

The next focal point of your pool rhythm is the transition between your last practice stroke and your actually hitting the cue ball. To go back to those apple-bobbers in your room, another thing you'll see them doing is rushing their strokes on tough pressure shots, especially when they're stroking from over an object ball. The first couple of their practice strokes might be fine, but suddenly there'll be this little flurry of activity. Some very good players do the same thing, simply because there are few players alive who can't be reached by pool's special pressures. And that's all it can be, in explaining that break from rhythm; since the little flurry of strokes adds absolutely nothing to the shot, whether successful or not, it can be due only to what's in the shooter's head.

Each player develops his own abilities, and tolerance, for the game's pressures, naturally. It's a matter of the peculiar combination of concentration and relaxation, and we'll be talking about each. And one good checkpoint for your own progress is, are you letting any shots intimidate you into rushing your stroke? *Your last practice stroke should always be the same as the rest.* The immediate benefit of this is that your actual stroke has a planned beginning, middle, and end;

all are imperative for both rhythm and an effective swing, whether in pool, tennis, baseball, golf, name it.

Now for the stroke itself. You've seen to it that you've made the necessary pause after your last practice stroke, and that is the last thing I want you to think about. Go right ahead and hit the cue ball exactly as you saw yourself doing in your mental rehearsals. It should not be necessary for you to think about any of the various aspects of your stroke, and may well in fact be harmful (unless, of course, you hit a slump, in which you should take some practice time to analyze *everything*). Take a backswing exactly like the one you saw yourself taking; hit the ball at just that rehearsed speed; follow through with the same smoothness. The first key to executing a smooth, rhythmic stroke is rehearsing one. Then just do it.

That brings us to your movement between shots. I'll assume that most of you have seen *The Hustler*; remember their first game and Fats's first turn at the table? Paul Newman's line was something close to, "Look how he moves, like a dancer." The author of that line, the late Walter Tevis, knew his pool. Good players have a rhythm so highly developed that they do in fact seem to be moving in a highly disciplined, almost choreographed way; and that's a critical part of what makes them so good. When a player like Lou "Machine Gun" Butera flies around a table at his well-known rack-a-minute pace, he is literally and figuratively stepping to a different drummer; that is the tempo the game suggests to him.

I can't encourage you to play that fast, and I tend to doubt that he would either. What makes more sense by far is for you to find a playing speed that feels comfortable, and do your best to stick to it. As I said before, when a player breaks his rhythm between open shots, it's usually an indication of trouble. Concentrate on playing without pause, as long as things are going according to plan for you.

The key word there is *open* shots. Certainly the game is going to make you stop and think; after all, I've already advised you to reexamine all layouts following break shots, and that's only one reason for interrupting your rhythm. Any time something does not go as you rehearsed it, or something happens that you could not possibly have rehearsed, that's a valid reason to break your shotmaking rhythm and take time to reexamine or remake your plan. And as we pointed out in the section on sequence, your first shot following such pauses should be the easiest one you can find that will lead you to another. Your rhythm should come back to you like Poe's raven.

Even in your short runs, try to move between shots at a consistent rhythm. The longer your runs become, naturally, the more you'll become aware of your rhythm during them. Don't slow down, unless you have a good reason to—and don't speed up, either. A good run really gets your adrenaline flowing if you're at all into the game, and your rate of play will automatically increase to some degree. But don't let yourself get carried away, because too much added speed in your rhythm invariably leads to mistakes, frequently quite simple ones.

Now and then, you'll find a between-shots dawdler who has become a top player in spite of that. As fine as these players are, I think it's fair to say that they are exceptions to the rule.

Dead Stroke—Pool's Magic Kingdom

Dead stroke is the commodity which advanced pool players enjoy for only a few minutes out of all the years they live, yet they willingly invest those years in pursuit of this magical state. You probably hear the expression almost as often as you play (assuming you play with and around competitive players; that alone can influence your improvement). If you're fortunate enough to be able to watch good players often, you've probably seen a player in this blessed state of consciousness. If you're *really* fortunate, you may have fallen under its spell now and then yourself. Maybe you've even suffered the folly of trying to turn it on at will.

So how come you can't? And what *is* dead stroke, exactly?

This issue is pool's version of Stonehenge; nothing is likely to be resolved about it soon, and, like all magic, it was perhaps not meant to be explained in a once-and-for-all way. Let's begin this way: The expression refers to a state, or trance, rather than to anything you do with your cue. It will no doubt *incorporate* your perfect execution, but "dead stroke" has far more to do with your head. Particularly, it has to do with what psychologists term *left-brain* and *right-brain* activity.

We'll try to confine this discussion to its relevance to pool, so let's review its basics quickly: The *left* half of that incredible computer between your ears is the *rational* half, interpreting the world around you in terms of words and logical thoughts. It controls your powers of speech and all your rational processes, as well as the right half of your body. Without it, you couldn't even survive, much less play pool.

The *right* half, on the other hand, is your *creative* half. Oddly, you could survive without it, although life probably wouldn't be much fun. For our purposes, this is the half of your brain that has to do with how comfortable you feel in your stance, the firmness of your bridge, the solidness (or mellowness) of the cue-ball hit itself, and the cue-ball and object-ball speed. None of these factors can be measured very well in words; the left half of your brain, therefore, can't or won't accept the task, and the right half takes over. But just look at how critical those factors are to successful pool, and you begin to see the wisdom of this theory.

Stated another way, it's the left half of your brain that tells you to "make the 4-ball in the corner, with enough follow to go to the end rail and come out again for the 5-ball in the side." But it's the right half that measures the shot, rehearses it mentally, and then allows you to execute it as planned.

Now let's try two simple exercises that illustrate this phenomenon. These are *not* a direct and immediate path to dead stroke; they're merely an extremely simple application of a complex learning process. But I will suggest that you may notice a difference, and quite soon.

Exercise 1: Shoot a few balls (five, ten, or more) left-handed, or right-handed if you normally shoot left-handed. Set up some very simple, short shots that you can make with stop-ball position, or at least minimal cue-ball travel. If you feel a little antsy toward the end of this exercise, that means it's working perfectly for you so far.

Exercise 2: Set up the 1-, 2-, and 3-balls in a row in center table, one to two balls' width apart. Take the cue ball in hand, and using your normal shooting hand, shoot the balls in sequence into the same-side pocket. You should begin with just a very few degrees of angle on the 1, achieve the identical angle on the 2, and end up perfectly straight-in on the 3 to execute this exercise perfectly (although it can still be accomplished less than perfectly). Try to stay with center-draw, although a cue-tip's worth of English is permissible, too. Above all, *concentrate on the cue ball, not the object ball or pocket, with your eyes after cue-ball/object-ball contact.*

Neither of these drills should take more than a few minutes. Now go ahead and practice as you usually do, whether you begin with formal drills or just open balls on a table (I recommend formal drills). But add one more wrinkle: *Make it a point to chalk your cue with the hand you don't usually use.* What follows may not be your all-time greatest practice session, but if you've been disciplined enough to complete all three drills, I think you're eventually going to feel a difference that pleases you.

Why should this be? Because in sinking a few simple opposite-handed shots, you tap yourself into a side of the brian that isn't used to being called on that way. If the exercise made you feel slightly irritable or anxious, that was the side you *do* normally use, informing you it doesn't like being scorned. Chalking your cue with the opposite hand had the same effect. And the three-ball exercise, as simple as it was, actually got you in touch with all the sensations to be experienced while playing pool: stance, bridge, stroke, follow-through, pocketing a ball, and cue-ball control for correct position. It's identical to a golfer's warming up with very short putts rather than long drives. Any smart golfer will tell you that the former way is correct because the player takes on simple tasks to get in touch with the feel of stroking and scoring; golf and pool are more similar than you'd think. The dimension you added, of cue-ball focus after contact, got you to stop thinking about an extraneous element, one you can't control (the flight of the object ball), and instead invest your mental energy on the elements you can control (stroke execution and, indirectly, the cue ball). Thus you were focused on feeling the cue ball rather than the success of your shot. One is all feelings; the other is all words ("Is it going in? What if it doesn't? I'll miss. I'll lose." Does any of this sound familiar?). And feelings are exactly what you want to be in touch with if you're to have any hope of falling into dead stroke.

Does this mean that you want to abandon your left brain completely to play pool? No. Remember what Elaine said to Benjamin in *The Graduate*: "You have to have a plan, Benjamin. I don't want you to leave without a plan." The role of your left brain is to analyze things; thus it's your good friend as long as you're examining the table layout and forming your shot plan. But if you let it go on murmuring to you once you get into your shooting stance, you're up against the most formidable nemesis of your playing career. You must learn to shut the left brain down at just the right time—when you go into your shooting stance—in order to achieve dead stroke.

The state of dead stroke is not unlike a hypnotic trance, and several top players have worked with hypnotists in an effort to achieve it more readily. One hypnotherapist, Ryan Elliott of the suburban Chicago area, even specializes in helping pool players through hypnotism. Once you're good and under, you'll abandon your conscious shot-by-shot planning in favor of simply recognizing which ball to shoot next; if your right brain does take over completely, you'll lose track of how many you've run or what the score is or who's watching, because those are all verbal expressions.

Right-brain activity, remember, is nothing you have to tell yourself to do. It's the process by which you learn to ride a bicycle, or make those minute adjustments on the steering wheel when driving a car, or draw a picture, or walk, and so on. In pool, when your ring finger flutters as you form your bridge, that's an example of right-brain activity; your hand is automatically seeking out maximum firmness and comfort without your telling it to.

The really critical factors in achieving dead stroke are speed and concentration, and there are some other important aspects of play that will fall into line once you've accomplished those first two. But remember, my writing about this, and your reading my writing, are not enough to get you there. Reading and writing are two very pure functions of the left side of the brain, precisely what you must get away from in order to get to dead stroke.

Speed

A player in the throes of dead stroke is almost certainly hitting the balls at a different speed than he normally does. Whether that player adds or decreases speed in his stroke is a function of what feels best to him, even though less speed makes more sense intellectually. As his sensitivity and awareness increase, the player will have a feel not only for the cue ball's travels, but for its actual spin as well. The speed and spin he chooses will be the ideal complements for the angles of deflection that occur on all but straight-in shots; there is just no arguing that speed affects angles, thus results, in pool. And unless you're a physicist or engineer who measures stroke in terms of $E = MC^2$, PSI, and MPH, you must learn to put your faith in your right brain to select speed for you. You must learn to immerse yourself in the speed of the cue ball, which was the purpose of Exercise 2.

Concentration

Concentration is virtually inseparable from sense of speed. The first thing to learn is that telling yourself to concentrate, while a logical first step, is no substitute for the real thing, and in fact is ultimately what you do *not* want to do. Those solo pep talks, after all, can only take place in the form of your left brain's precious words, and dead stroke has nothing to do with words. Your pool concentration should instead help you keep your head down on your shots, follow through on your stroke, and get your cue tip closer to the cue ball than you normally do as you address each shot (which enhances your hitting the cue ball precisely where you want to; some even make it a point to look for the cue tip's reflection in the cue ball's finish). Another feeling many top players enjoy is shortening their bridge until the backswing actually brings the tip of the cue into the loop of their thumb and forefinger. You'll also recognize proper shot sequences even though the ball you're shooting and your next few shots may have no geometrical relationship whatsoever that can be put into words.

But you'll be much, much closer to all of that if you can just immerse yourself in the cue ball. That's really what the entire game of pool, in any form, is all about. Why is that thought process relevant to dead stroke? Because to tap in to the right half of your brain and begin to play the game by feel, you've got to minimize the inputs of the left half of your brain. When you're really focused on that lone white ball, you're telling your left brain to kiss off (no pun intended); all your left brain can tell you about the cue ball is that it's small, round, and white. But if you expand your concentration to include the object balls, you're leaving yourself wide open to all those poisonous speculations (Will I pocket this? What if I don't?) till you're a mumbling, unconfident mess, fumbling vaguely for your bankroll and cursing your karma. Once you're into stance, you must reduce your thinking to concentrating on the basics: cue-ball location and the feel of the shot.

Forget About Perfection

To ignore this suggestion is to risk going bonkers. You simply cannot achieve dead stroke at will; that kind of mind control challenges even yogi masters and is beyond anything more than the occasional grasp of mortal man. Even the world's greatest players can only reach dead stroke part of the time, and none can be sure of sustaining it for any length of time.

Shut Out the Voices

Most of what we've discussed already deals with shutting out the voice of your own left brain. In an important money or tournament match, that lone voice can easily turn into the Mormon Tabernacle Choir, with each member singing a different song. The cue-ball concentration techniques we discussed previously will help. So will concentrating on your breathing. You've got to go beyond that, though, and shut out outside distractions, too. That doesn't mean that you must metamorphose into an antisocial creep; it means that you simply have to recognize that talking, laughing, and kibitzing are potential risks to your game.

Finally, even when you've mastered the knack of shutting out your own negative thoughts and voices, don't fall into the trap of congratulating yourself either. I wish I had a buck for every player I've seen run 50 or 60 in a 100-point game then sit around reveling in glory while the other guy got to 100 first. Remember, any judgments on how well you're playing or how many balls you've run will take the form of words, and you know by now what part of the brain those words come from. Congratulate yourself once you've taken your cue apart.

Forget Your Opponent

Pool, properly played, should be approached like golf, in that you should merely play *the game*, not your opponent. The game itself is competition enough. Unless your opponent has a known weakness you can play to (safeties, banks, long shots, etc.), disregard the mental dossier: whom he's beaten, how many racks he's run, how many games he's won, etc. Don't listen to it. Stated another way, dead stroke and a faceless opponent are a matched set.

How Does It Feel?

I'm not quoting the great Bob Dylan lyric, merely reprising my earlier suggestion that you get in touch with, and anticipate the feel of, your cue against the cue ball. Whatever your preference in cue-joint material, get used to that feel and dwell on it while you are addressing your shot.

Follow Through

Follow-through is not only essential for optimal stroke execution, but an excellent focal point for concentration. **Specifically, you** should visualize not only the area between your cue tip and cue ball, but the area beyond the cue ball that you'll need for your follow-through as well. Some articulate players claim they visualize the entire cue/cue-ball/object-ball sequence as a puzzle to be solved: The shot executed at the correct speed unlocks the door, and the object ball magically disappears down a hole. Some players are so adept at this visualization of stroke that they dip the tip of the cue down past the side of the cue ball nearest them and instead fit in at the ball's vertical axis, down where the ball actually meets the cloth. (But I can't recommend you try this. You risk fouling, and besides, you can't hit the ball down there; why not aim someplace where you can hit the ball?)

Practice with a Metronome

You may want to try this tip (and the next one) in private, unless you don't mind a few snickers. But it works. A good metronome costs around $30 at any music supply store; besides providing a great basis for concentration, it will help you find your optimum playing rhythm by making you aware of the rhythm (or lack of rhythm) in your play. Every sport, except possibly golf, involves its own rhythm, and pool is no different. If you have good rhythm for music and/or dancing, that's an advantage, but it's no guarantee. Pool rhythm is a complex subject all in itself.

Practice with a Headset

And, while we're at it, practice while listening to sung music. Music with lyrics is better than instrumental; lyrics will provide a diversion for your left brain. They help your rhythm, too. Try to remain aware of the stereo separation.

The gist of all this is to suggest that you're capable of playing *much* better than you do now, maybe even better than you ever thought you could. Unless and until you achieve the magical dead-stroke state, you will probably not be able to approximate just what your real potential is. Besides, dead stroke will teach you something about the wisdom of observing rather than judging, which will serve you well in all the rest of your life.

Go and be great.

Relaxation

So much for your head; what about your bod?

Well, it *should* be another aspect of what we've been talking about all along: *fluidity*. I started out by suggesting that you hit the balls more softly, so as to increase your smoothness. Throughout the book, we've seen the benefits of fluid, continuous thinking ahead of yourself. Rhythm and fluidity are just about synonymous, right? Well, I think you'll find it impossible, in any physical endeavor, to be fluid and rigid at the same time (unless you count sex, and there you are again, with lust in your soul when I want you thinking pool). Contract the muscle of your choice, keep it that way, and try to accomplish any natural movement smoothly. Other muscles will usually begin to tighten in sympathy, either slowing you down drastically or making you jerky. Now *relax* and try the same move. Feel the difference?

The reason for this section in the first place is that relaxation in pool is admittedly easier to talk about than achieve. And, again, your powers of relaxation, just like those of concentration, largely have to do with what's in your head. Concentration and relaxation would seem to be at odds with one another; yet I think you'll find that in pool, they actually feed each other.

You can test this quite easily. Next time you miss a ball, in practice or otherwise, think of me and freeze (as people often do). Aren't you tight someplace, right this second? Most likely, in your stroking hand, but maybe in your back or neck or legs or gut or all of the above? Some of that will be an involuntary reaction to your seeing the missed shot on its errant way; but the chances are that some of it was there for your stroke, too.

I've seen the game played at the highest level the world has to offer, and I can't think of a single level at which you totally get away from the expression, "He choked." Ring-around-the-collar runs rampant in the game, or at least its reputation does. Everybody is accused of choking. You can still turn up guys who'll swear that Mosconi choked. *Mosconi!* For me, it was like being told there was no Santa Claus.

It's certainly true that the vast majority of players do choke to some degree. At least, that's what they do emotionally. What they do physically is *clench* something, somewhere in their bods. That has to happen first.

Let's check the basics of your game and see if we can help you let go.

Begin with your stance. As I've said, *how* you stand doesn't concern me a lot as long as your stance isn't actually wrong, and other books have instructed you well on that. If they've omitted anything, it's the importance of being comfortable in your stance. There is no point in imitating the stance of anyone if that stance doesn't feel as good to you as it looks good on the player you're emulating. It's just that the stance of your choice must accomplish two things: balance, plus the opportunity to keep your cue level. How low you should be in that stance has to do with the characteristics of your own body, more than with any advice I could give you. I do think that the ability to get down *good* and low—but comfortably—is a decided advantage.

Comfort is the key, simply because you can't possibly be relaxed unless you're comfortable first. It can be a factor of your balance as well as your stance. You can inadvertently put that front foot down somewhere you usually don't and wreak havoc with the shot, if not your whole game. It's because your misstep altered your balance, which made you uncomfortable, and unless you stopped right then to check everything out, it was discomfort cutting into your shot, nothing else.

Good balance feels good, both in your body and in your head. It's probably the first ingredient of pool confidence. Your balance, whatever foot position you use to achieve it, should be enough that you could resist a theoretical push on your shooting side. Leave your elbow free enough that you can take your cue back and stroke forward in a level plane, and you have the fundamentals of a perfect stroke. And the ultimate starting point was relaxation.

As to relaxation of the stroke itself, it's quite similar to the point we began with in the book. Just as the correct speed for any given shot is the minimum speed that will get the work done, the correct tension for you to apply to the cue butt is the *minimum* tension with which you can still control a beginning, middle, and end to every stroke. Too light, of course, and you'd have lots of minijavelins in your game, but I don't think you'll have to worry about gripping the cue too light. Too *tight* is much more common, and that's what you want to watch out for.

As you probably know by now, you can't draw the cue ball unless your butt hand is relaxed. But it's more important than that: The same cue ball, stroked in precisely the same spot at the same speed, will react in two quite different ways when stroked first with a relaxed hand and then with a clenched one. Try any medium-to-hard shot both ways and see.

And then, start working on a lighter grip. That's where your touch for the game will come from. If you've ever heard a pool player praised for his "soft touch," the words refer to more than his cue-ball control. If you can efficiently execute your stroke with a grip of a third less tension than you were using before, you can expect your cue-ball control to increase by at least that much, quite likely more.

The starting point here, again, was relaxation. It is not possible to hold your cue lightly with an unrelaxed hand.

Yet despite all this logic, all but a handful of players on earth could still trace missed shots to something that was clenched. They all do it, and it's hard to say why, because when you get right down to it, hardly anything that's good in life has much to do with clenching.

Ever been on a bad blind date? I'll bet my last dime that you spent a good part of it clenching. (To be fair about it, your date probably did, too.)

Ever been late somewhere when it really mattered whether you were on time? Terrific clenching spot.

Been to a dentist lately? The very words probably made you clench just now.

Sometimes the humor goes out of it. Show me a case of hypertension and I'll show you a postgraduate clencher.

Clenching. Who needs it? Boxers, maybe, and others whose physical endeavors involve normal muscle contractions. But at the pool table, it's the last thing you want to do, and it's no bargain anywhere else.

How do you stop? Largely with your head. Physically, I've had some luck with a technique that involves consciously relaxing the base of my spine and the base of my tongue. I find that if I'm relaxed there, everything else falls into line. You may have had an Army sergeant or other mentor who suggested that you maintain sphincteral tightness, but that achievement won't do you a bit of good in the game of pocket billiards. Nor, in my experience, away from the game either.

As for your head, I think relaxation has a lot to do with your perspective on the game. You may be overestimating the importance of a given shot to the entire game; you may be overestimating the importance of the game itself.

Regarding the first, every pool game in history that went two or more innings can be traced to the losing player's miss at one point or another; but that hardly means that the game hinges on *every* ball you shoot, unless your opponent is the obnoxious sort who is always a threat to run out. He's probably something less than that. And since you've got the table all to yourself, why not keep it a little longer? You'll do that once you've convinced yourself to shoot the balls you know you should, rather than simply the ones you fear least. Don't let the balls make up your mind for you; they are unqualified to do that. Select the right shot; hit it with the most level, relaxed stroke you can; if you miss, you miss. You'll get another chance.

And when a missed shot *does* cost you the game, what happens then? The San Andreas fault will not let go (not yet, anyway), nor will any other natural disasters occur. Banks and schools will still be open on the next available day. It's just a game, and despite your losing it you may still be pretty sure that somehow it will still get to be tomorrow.

I can hear those who know me sniggering at this point, so the rest of you might as well hear it from the horse's, er, mouth: I was a cuebuster of the first stripe for a good many moons. What got me over it, and it was no cinch, were the simultaneous realizations that the cues were both good and expensive; turning them into driftwood still did

not put the missed ball in the subway; it really didn't make me feel
any better, even though I thought it would; and what it did make me
feel and look like was the village idiot. So I stopped. Sounds simplis-
tic, I know, but you can see only what you let yourself see.

I'm not so hypocritical as to suggest that I oppose the playing of
pool for stakes. All I'm saying is that the stakes should not only be
affordable, but *comfortable*, in that they create no artificial pressure
that will detract from your enjoyment of the game. Personally, I generally play with guys my speed, or slightly better; I try to handicap
the game, when necessary, as fairly as I can; sometimes I win, sometimes I lose, but in neither case does the GNP move in the slightest.

It's also quite possible, and highly recommended, that you relax
when your opponent is at the table too. Or at least, to do that until
game ball is within reach in your next inning, at which point you could
be forgiven if you began to psych yourself up instead. The price good
players pay for being that good is that they never let up on themselves
in the chair; the game is always within their single-inning capabili-
ties, and it must be a never-ending pep talk. (I wouldn't know.) But I
think they'd still be more comfortable relaxing.

Put your cue aside; lean it where it won't fall. (Holding on to it will
only offer you another clenching opportunity.) Try to learn from what
your opponent is doing, rather than hating him for it. (It's a good idea
to forget whom you're playing. My opponents all seem to.) There is
growing support for the technique of concentrating on your breathing
as a technique of relaxation; at the table or in the seat, this will also
help keep your mind from wandering. It would be great if you could
train yourself to think about a breath or two every time a negative pool
thought popped into your head, especially when planning sequences.

Relaxation will help you play better pool, because you're enjoying it
more. Or maybe it's the other way around. It doesn't matter.

The W. P.'s Revisited

Let's return to the table.

Your w. p.'s will always serve you well in helping you simplify
the game, and that's what advanced play is all about. The more

religiously you adhere to them, the better your results should be. But w. p., remember, stands for "*Whenever Possible*," which obviously means that they're not always going to be possible. Before we conclude this Straight-Pool chapter by turning you loose to think your way correctly through two racks, it probably would be helpful to review the w. p.'s and examine both typical violations and their consequences, and typical exceptions to the rule.

We'll skip over w. p.'s 1 and 2 (that is shoot soft, avoid unnecessary English); they are so fundamental to the game as to defy diagramming or examples. All I ask is that you always bear them in mind.

W. p. 3 deals with the importance of not moving secondary object balls that don't need to be moved. This will come up as early in the game as on your first shot following your opponent's break; chances are you'll have a long shot to deal with, and another shot or two available once you've made that long one. There will usually be something you can

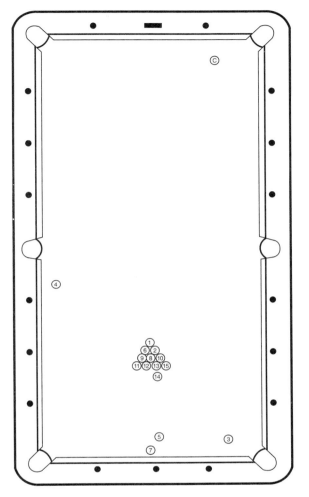

Diagram 71.

do to use one of those open balls as a D-ball, to open or partially open the remaining clustered balls and launch a good run . . . provided that you don't miss *and* you can leave your early open shots as they lie.

In Diagram 71, the balls have just been broken at the outset of the game. This is a reasonably typical leave, with two long shots available right now and a rebreaking opportunity in those loose balls behind the stack.

Of course the 3-ball is easier to pocket in this spot than the 4. But your angle to the 3-ball makes it quite likely that you'll move one or both of the loose balls down near the bottom rail too. And unless you can be absolutely sure of where the moved object ball *and* the cue ball will end up, your chances are excellent for obliterating your secondary break shot opportunity and shutting your run down at 1, hardly a critical factor in the game.

Since pocketing the 3-ball nets you the *certainty* of that one lone point, wouldn't it be smarter to shoot the 4, which will cough up *three* certainties if pocketed with correct speed? Individually, it's a tougher shot than the 3, but you're supposed to be looking further ahead than that. Pocketing the 4 will leave your cue ball near the middle of the table, with a near-straight shot on the 3 and easy access to either the 5 or the 7. The 5-ball, of course, is a D, and if you don't like your position for it following the 3, the 7 will even act as a safety valve. If you decide you don't have the break shot you want on the 5 going right, you can still use the 7 to position yourself on the 5 going left; it's a D-ball in either direction. If you either overcut or undercut the 4, too bad, but you don't figure to leave very much; the cue ball will be very near the stack. The only danger here, and I think the benefits make it a worthwhile risk, lies in leaving the 4-ball very near the pocket—"hanging"—if you miss; correct cue-ball speed is partial insulation against that (even though the possibility can never be *completely* eliminated).

Here's another common example of the exact same principle. Diagram 72 shows you a set-up with some of the object balls already off the table; the shooter needs only pocket the 1-ball and follow out for position on the 2. That will lead to the 3, or the 4, both good D's. But in Diagram 73, the player has nudged the 3-ball on his way out, even though there was

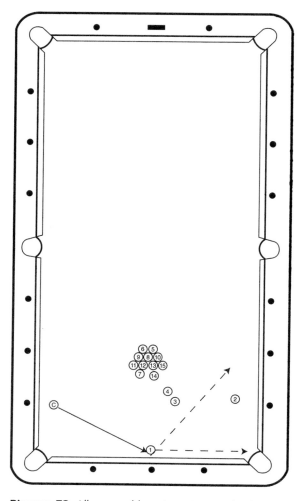

Diagram 72. All we need here is position on the 2.

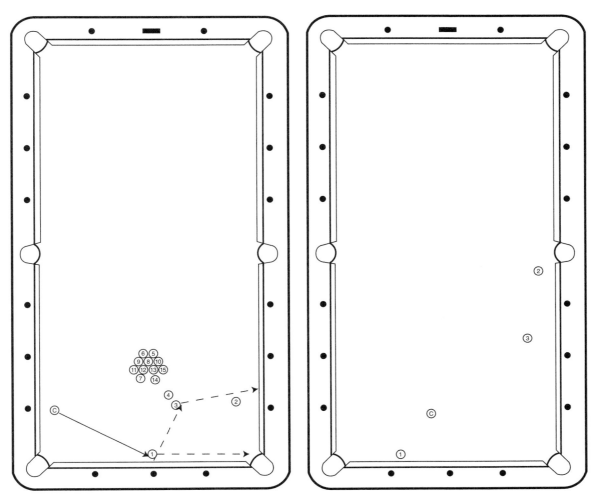

Diagram 73.   **Diagram 74.**

plenty of room; this will often be a matter of a hair too much speed, because speed unquestionably affects pool angles. At any rate, you can see the dismal consequences, even though he barely moved the 3 an inch: no shots *anywhere*. Touching a secondary object ball without purpose made all the difference. Even the most subtle violations of w. p. 3 can turn a game around. You'll see this in the next game you watch, regardless of how good the players are.

Diagram 74 offers a reasonable example of the rape of w. p. 4, don't drive the cue ball when you can roll it. Only a thin rail cut shot on the 1 stands between the shooter and a very good key-ball/break-ball duo, the 2 and 3. This is as good a time as any to pass along a sim-

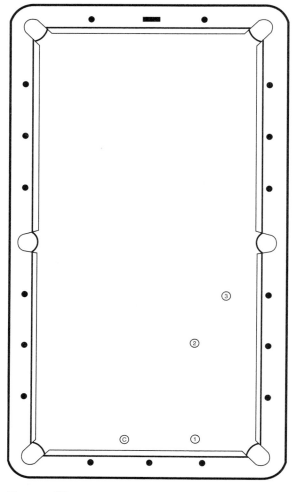

Diagram 75.

ple, single-sentence tip that can improve your overall game virtually overnight: *learn to stop overhitting thin cut shots.* The vast majority of pool players think that because a thin object ball hit is required, it will take increased cue-ball speed to get the object ball where it's going. That is simply not true, except for the very thinnest cut shots in the game, those close to 90 degrees, where the actual point of contact between the two balls is in fact slightly smaller than on other shots. But most thin cut shots require no more than medium speed to make them, and if you can master this you will enjoy both increased accuracy and cue-ball control, plus the confidence that comes with them.

With respect to Diagram 74, what most players will do here is drive their cue ball up and part way down the length of the table, trying to pocket the 1 and get position for the 2 in the corner. It takes a polished player to merely roll the 1 into the corner and stick around for the 2 in the side instead, but that's the right shot. The other way, you're sacrificing accuracy, begging the 1-ball to hang because of overspeed, and not even ensuring good position for the 2 in the corner. Roll the stone. Don't drive it. It will reward your gentleness. And make it a point to practice soft-hitting thin cut shots. You'd be surprised at how little speed it takes to get the job done.

Diagram 75 shows you the work of a player who's been minding his w. p.'s & q's, so to speak; those last three balls lie pretty near ideally, with an easy shot on the 1, followed by natural position on the 3, and a subsequent break shot on the 2. But oh my stars and garters, look what happened to him in Diagram 76. No position, no break shot, no *shot* for that matter, and how did he wreak this havoc? Well, by hitting the 2, of course; but he wouldn't have hit the 2 at all if he had avoided driving his cue ball to the rail. He misread the angle of the cue ball off the 1, or applied a tad more spin than he meant to, and cue-ball action off a rail will amplify those kinds of errors. Our player has pillaged w. p. 5 (don't go to a rail unnecessarily) and justice has been sure and swift in this case. All he had to do was pocket the 1 with a soft, firm draw, and he'd have easily cleared the 2 for position on the 3. This is not a rare mistake by any means; learn to watch out for it in your game. The rails can be your good friends in advanced pool, but for some stuffy reason they insist that you use them correctly before they accept your friendship. Most of the game's bad luck seems to accrue to shots where the cue ball comes off at least one rail. It's downright spooky.

If you buy that, it shouldn't be any trouble to sell you on w. p. 6, choose one-rail routes rather than two-railers. The shots in the game that make best use of two-rail cue-ball routes are those involving pocketing at the head of the table. In that instance, going two rails with the cue ball makes sense, because it creates a natural angle toward the center of the table. But back at the business end of the table, there are recurring two-rail route situations that can give you fits, especially those where the object ball is near a pocket and not quite straight-in with the cue ball (Diagram 77). Most players will elect to drive the cue ball through the object ball and off those two rails to come farther up the table. There's no question that that can be made to work, but it takes more cue-ball control than you think; the reason for that is that rails take the most wear down there near the pocket, and are therefore at their least predictable there. You may

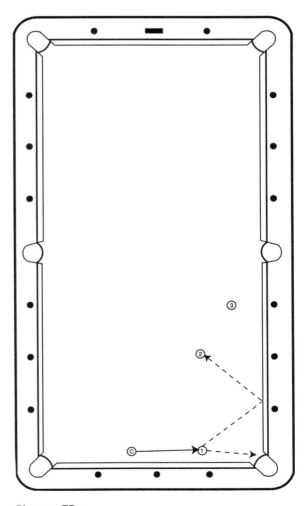

Diagram 76.

well get a far sharper angle than you bargained for, if the cue ball skids at all.

Unless you're backed up against a rail (and the cue ball isn't, in the above diagram), you don't have to risk that. You can chop a shot like that in, dead center ball, no wrist action, no follow-through, so the cue ball goes to the bottom rail with no English whatsoever; that is a shot the rail can respect, and your reward is a prim, predictable cue-ball path out of there, parallel to the side rail (Diagram 78). Any time you can choose between this shot and Diagram 77's shot and still accomplish what you want to, go for 78.

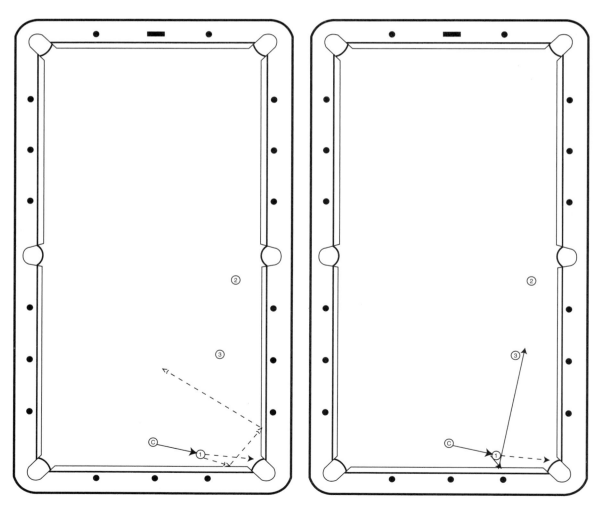

Diagram 77. Possible but risky.   **Diagram 78.** Possible and safe.

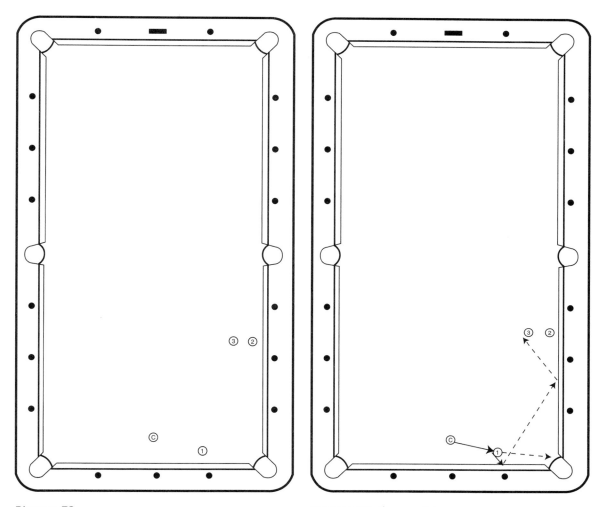

Diagram 79.

Diagram 80. The uncertain way.

Players who *choose* two-rail routes when they don't have to, and there are more of them than you think, are often players who use too much English as well, thus incurring double jeopardy for crimes against w. p. 6 *and* w. p. 2. It's a case of one bad habit feeding on another one, and these players pay some wicked dues, in the forms of exotic scratches, open-table stymies that should be photographed and placed in a time capsule, and all kinds of sundry cue-ball surprises.

Here comes Fancy Dan now, in Diagram 79. He's going to finesse the 1, get on the 2, and roll it up in the head corner, following right past the 3 for break-shot position. (At least he knows enough not to force his cue ball for position on the *other* side of the 2; that would

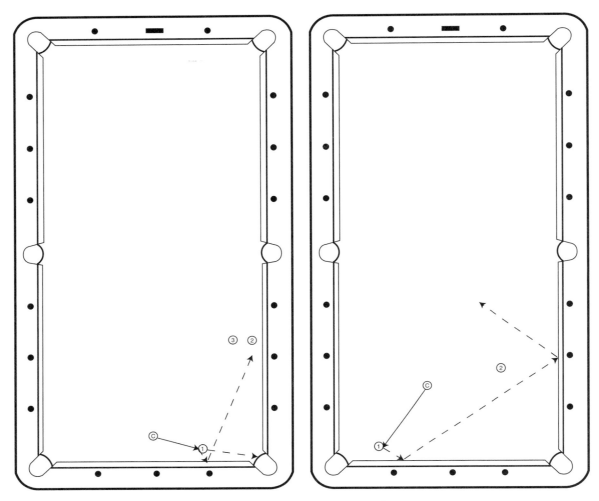

Diagram 81. More certain.   **Diagram 82.** The uncertain way.

be carnage against w. p. 4 into the bargain, and the game is not lenient with triple offenders.)

The catch is that he couldn't resist that pretty little *two*-rail route down there in the corner, as you see in Diagram 80. So he goosed up for some extra left-hand English, more than he needed, which caused him to overhit the shot and spin right into the Twilight Zone there where he can't use the 2 to get on the 3 anymore. It's not a total disaster; he can still pocket the 3 for position on the 2, but it's a far inferior break shot to the one he could have had. And you want to try to avoid giving away edges like that.

Diagram 81 shows what he should have done: little or no English, just a gentle stroke, above-center hit on the cue ball, nice pure follow-through, and a *one*-rail route. That way, the cue ball is moving *toward* the angle you want, rather than counter to it; and as long as your speed is okay, you can't go wrong.

Here's another common two-rails-instead-of-one error, in Diagram 82. Players will frequently spin their cue ball two rails behind the break ball they're trying to leave. But they're risking hitting that ball on the way out, or going too far for a really efficient break-shot angle, due to the increased speed and spin they've employed. This shot should be played off the bottom rail *only* wherever you can, and it will be possible, as in Diagram 83, whenever the angle to the bottom rail off the key ball is generally parallel to the side rail. Just add a modest amount of reverse (right-hand in this case) English to negate your

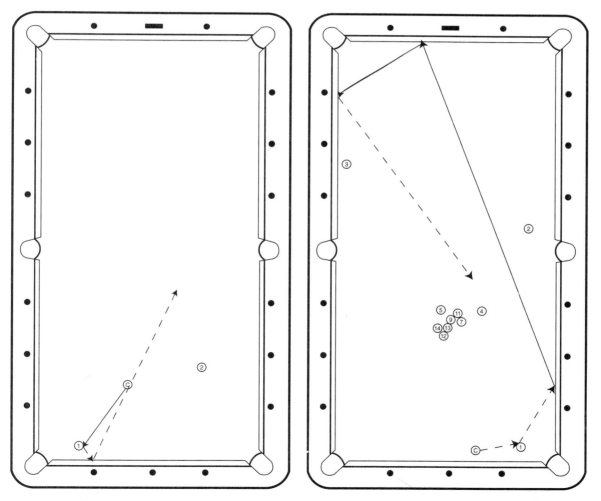

Diagram 83. The certain way.

Diagram 84. Here's the shot the way you see it.

angle, and your cue ball will walk right out there for a short, sure break shot.

The *three*-rail cue-ball routes that w. p. 7 wants you to shun generally begin with a thin cut shot into either corner pocket from behind the stack (Diagram 84). It looks like you won't be able to hold your cue ball in the area because of the angle, and because of that, normal speed will carry you uncomfortably far up the table; so you'd better drive your cue ball three rails and get back down to the balls that way.

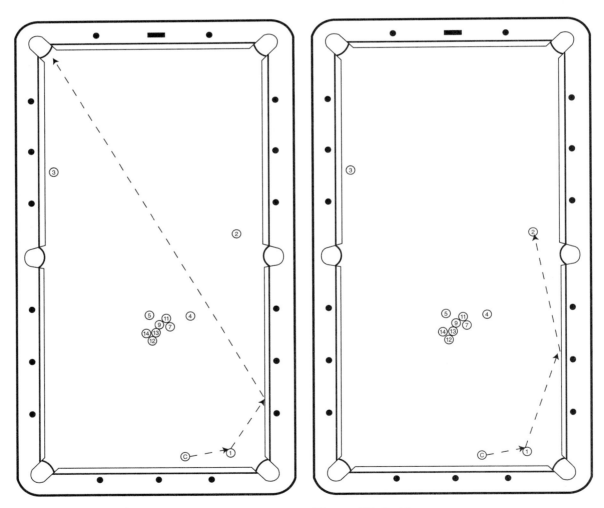

Diagram 85. Here's what can go wrong.   **Diagram 86.** Or this.

Which is quite possible, of course, but it takes an expert to spot all the things that can go wrong with the shot, and that's why the shot should be left to experts.

Pitfall 1: You never get to the second rail (Diagram 85). This happens (and it happens a lot) when the player misreads his angle off the rail, his cue-ball speed, his hit on the cue ball itself, or a combination of those. What happens is that the player creates a shorter angle for himself with his violation of stroking fundamentals, and the cue ball never gets the natural running English he was planning on and rehearsing to complete the angle he wanted. The cue ball actually curves into the corner pocket here (if that's any consolation), because of the shortened-angle effect.

Pitfall 2: You have a wreck with that 2-ball up yonder, that you never thought would even figure in the shot. Ah, but that 2-ball is in effect "bigger" than it looks; it's actually three balls wide, in that it can be contacted at either of its extreme edges or any point in be-

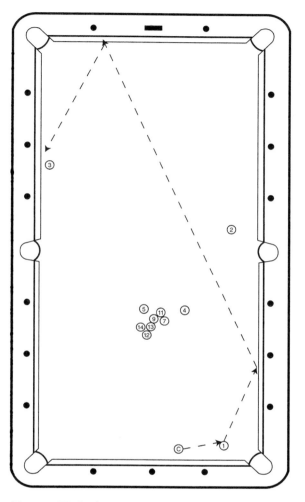

Diagram 87. Or this.

tween them. And if you do complete this unhappy little billiard and touch that ball at all, you're an odds-on favorite for punishment. (Diagram 86).

Pitfall 3: You don't quite make the third rail, because you didn't read the angle of your shot quite right and that straggling 3-ball up there gotcha (Diagram 87).

You get the idea. Pass up this shot unless you read it as an absolute must; and in that case, make sure you chart the course of your cue ball as thoroughly as you can. The highways are fraught with marauders out there.

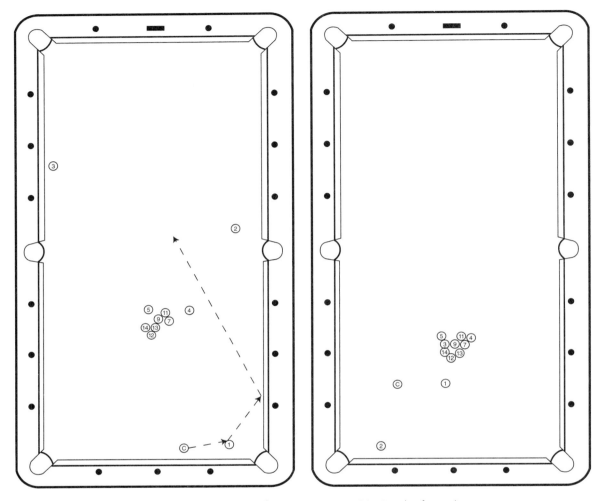

Diagram 88. But none of these things can happen if you just do this. Use some reverse (right-hand) English.

Diagram 89. Good safety valve.

To replace the shot with something of value, I refer you back to w. p. 4 (why drive when you can roll?) and the latest nugget of knowledge I offered a few paragraphs ago. Learn to hit your thin cut shots more softly.

Take another look at Diagram 84. If our player can instead muster the confidence to *roll* the object ball, he actually has a much better chance of approaching center table, and in a lot more predictable way. Some reverse, or "kill" English, and a slightly tighter cue grip are permissible when the angle on the cue ball is extremely thin. There is minimal danger here, the chance of scratching in the opposite side pocket, but you can guard against that with cue-ball speed alone once you develop the confidence to roll your thin cuts. Just like a good player has done in Diagram 88.

We've already seen why w. p. 8, the safety-valve notion, makes good sense. It lets you hit your secondary break shots softer, more smoothly, and more confidently, besides offering itself as a certainty. Remember, of course, that your break shot has to be in a direction *away* from your safety-valve ball (Diagrams 89 and 90); otherwise you have no assurance that nothing will come between the two of you.

Obviously, the most logical type of shot to select for a safety-valve ball is one that can be pocketed easily from just about anywhere, therefore a ball near a pocket. Advanced players, however, are able to preserve safety-valve situations out in the middle of action, and the balls they save for this function are even more versatile, because multiple pockets are available to them. It makes for some of the prettiest, most effortless sequences you'll ever see in the game, but it's nothing you'd ever fall into through serendipity. That ability, when shown against you, is an unmistakable sign that you've got some meaningful competition.

We can take a look at one example of that. Diagram 91 shows you the balls blasted to hell and gone, all A's and B's, nothing but multiple shots everywhere you look. The kind of rack, in short, that drives many intermediate-and-sometimes-even-better players into incoherence, because it's a lot harder than it looks. With all those loose balls occupying all that space, how are you going to

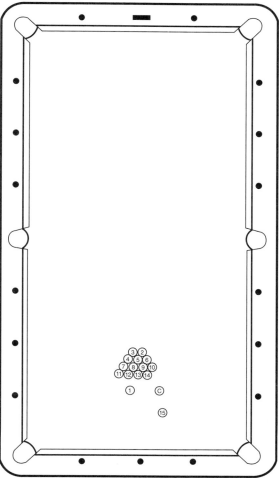

Diagram 90.

move your cue ball around? Haven't you been reading your w. p. 3? We don't want to move open balls, and that's all there seems to be. So whither?

Well, first consider what the 1, 2, 4, and 5 balls have in common. Of all the remaining balls, they are nearest to the four corners of the table, or, for lack of a more convenient term, they are "corner-most." There will always be balls you can designate this way, no matter how many balls are left or how they lie; and which ones they are is quite important, because of the individual two-ball relationships between them.

I think you'll find that if you can plan and execute sequences involv-

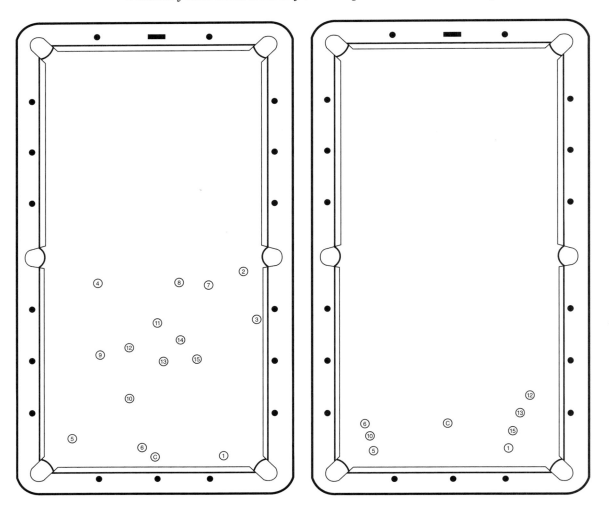

Diagram 91. An open rack.   **Diagram 92.**

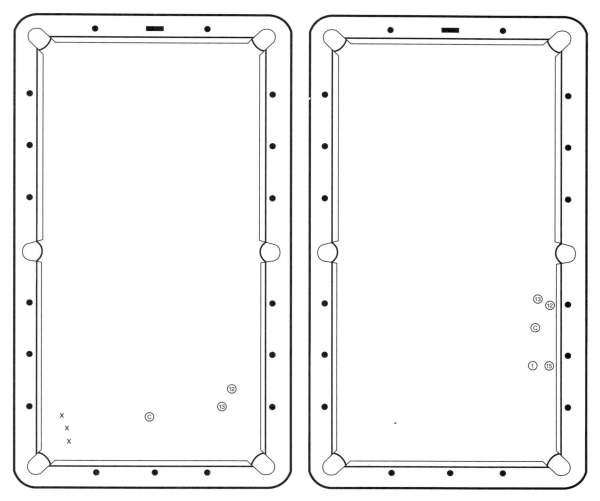

Diagram 93.   **Diagram 94.**

ing the consecutive pocketing of cornermost balls, the results will please you. You'll be working from the outside in, which is always recommended, and you'll be observing w. p. 3 devoutly. Like every other aspect of the game, this will not always be possible for you to do, but try to make it happen whenever you see the opportunity.

Diagram 91 represents that kind of opportunity, and here's how it should be exploited: The entire rack can be run without ever touching a second ball, simply by shooting a cornermost ball every shot. The balls are numbered in rotation to show you how the principle extends. Each ball, at the time it was struck, was cornermost relative to the rest of the remaining balls. Thus the player recognized a two-

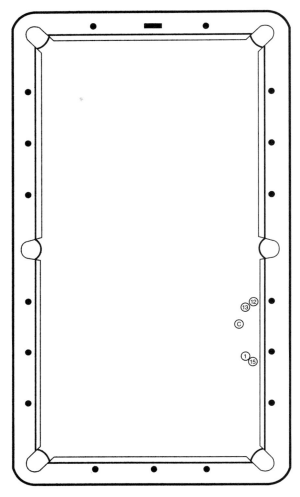

Diagram 95.

ball relationship between cornermost balls in each case. Learn to look for those relationships and where they might lead you. Chances are it will be into an excellent sequence.

This is nothing more than a highly advanced extension of the safety-valve principle. What we left alone, and saved till we needed it most, was our critical key-ball/break-ball sequence from the 9-ball on up.

So look for "Corner-To-Corner" possibilities to get you started when you're stuck for planning a sequence. And as long as we're bandying idioms about, another safety-valve premise you should learn is something I call "One From Column A, One From Column B" (and no, it doesn't mean that an hour after trying it you feel like playing again).

In Diagram 92 you see a very happy state of affairs: the cue ball midway between sets of A-balls for either corner pocket. The temptation is there to pocket balls consecutively in one corner, then come back and get the rest. Resist the temptation staunchly. You're much better off taking one from the right, then one from the left, then back again. That will offer you multiple safety-valve opportunities. If you took off all the balls on the right, for instance, and you got slightly out of line pursuing the balls on the left, as in Diagram 93, you'd wish you had left something on the other side. (While we're about this, keep in mind that when multiple balls are available to the same pocket, as in Diagram 92, you'll do well to shoot the middle balls in the row first. It will increase your cue-ball options later.)

That leaves the oft-taught w. p. 9, get balls off the rail early. Diagram 94 shows you a typical penalty for violation, and a mild one at that, because the balls you see are still pocketable even though they'll restrict your cue ball and decrease your options. A setup like you see here should be treated in the manner of One From Column A, One From Column B. But it's equally likely you'll suffer the boils of Diagram 95, where you'll have to rearrange your entire sequence to break up those miserable little bunches, with neither offering any safety-valve possibilities to the other until broken. Get to know your along-the-rail cut shots, thin and otherwise, so you can hit them confidently *when* you should as well as where you should.

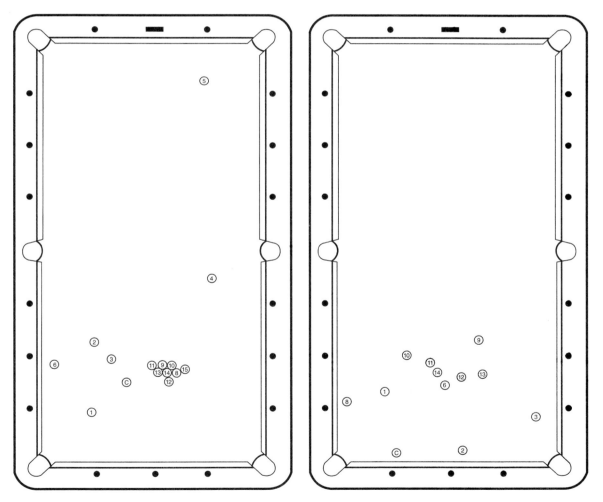

Diagram 96. A sequence of 1-2-3 will break up the cluster.

Diagram 97.

Which Ball?

Time to get down to cases. The following diagrams ask you to determine which ball(s) you'd shoot where, and why, to apply what you've learned so far. Some will offer clues, and some of the clues will be *false* clues (leading to ineffective and inappropriate solutions), to be interpreted as you see fit. My solutions follow the diagrams, but try coming up with your own solutions first before reading mine. It will help you learn to solve your own problems in your game.

The 1-2-3 sequence proposed in Diagram 96 is a false clue that a lot of players seem to delude themselves with. A better pattern than 1-2-3 here would be 1-4-5-6-2-3. You'll still break the cluster, but you'll have disposed of open balls which hold no great advantage as they lie, as well as the troublesome rail-ball 6. And you'll be breaking the clustered balls into open space, which means far less risk of new mini-clusters.

Diagram 97 actually embodies several of the position-play concepts we've considered so far. You'd correctly begin by shooting the 2-ball, but the proper next shot, and one which might fool many players, is the 8 (see the discussion of "cornermost" balls starting on page 118). You can achieve position on the 8 either with follow on the cue ball, or with inside draw. The 8 should get you somewhere advantageous for the 10 in the opposite-side pocket, and that shot should be used to get you to the narrow window where you can play the 14 in the corner; the 14 unlocks the rest of the rack and allows you to save the 9 and 13 as your key ball and next-rack break shot, respectively.

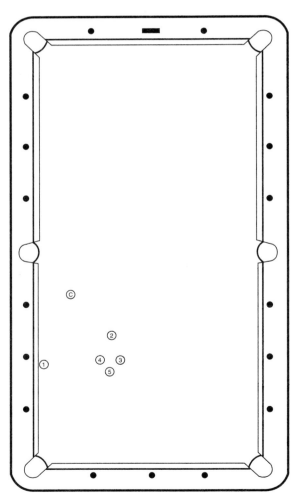

Diagram 98. Nudge apart the 3-4-5 and you'll have a fine break shot left.

You're probably catching on by now: In Diagram 98, that three-ball cluster, once you look closely enough, doesn't need any nudging. You can save an easy, juicy break shot by merely shooting the balls in numerical order, without your cue ball ever touching a second object ball. Again, these clues are included not to trick you, but to demonstrate how many players trick themselves. Be smarter than that.

You should have the solution to Diagram 99 down cold, even though this is a genuine toughie. Of course you can blow the stack away with a dead 8-4-5 combination. But don't. Instead, go around the horn numerically, 1-2-3; use the 8 as a modest break shot of its own, coming back to use the still-dead 4-5 to break the remaining clustered balls in the other direction. Your reason for doing that is to get more uniform distribution of the broken balls, which often leads to those delicious, effortless stop-ball sequences. And, you generally leave one or more balls in the immediate vicinity of the rack, ideal for break shots into the next frame.

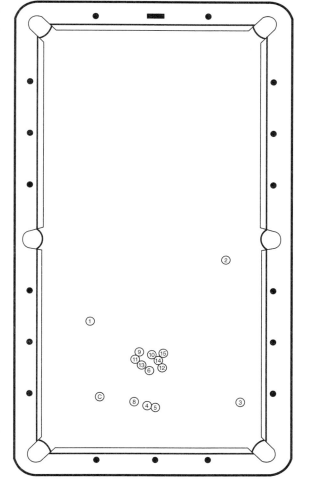

Diagram 99. The 8-4-5 is "dead" into the corner.

These dilemmas, and the process for ferreting out the optimal solution, are probably fodder for a whole new book in themselves. New ones will probably present themselves to you every single time you play or practice, and that's really what makes the game such titanic fun: The rolls are just about never the same. What makes you better equipped than your next opponent to take on these problems is that you now have the proper background in position-play rules of thumb. Remember, unless you've already achieved dead stroke, it won't do merely to randomly choose a ball to shoot; be sure of your reasons for your shot selection. It might feel like all that reasoning will take you ages, but trust me, eventually it will come to you instantaneously.

Some Practice Drills

Many of America's best-known pool teachers are in agreement that when it comes to this game, the age-old "Practice makes perfect" doesn't make nearly as much sense as "Perfect practice makes perfect."

In fact, what is probably the most common method of practice is also probably the least efficient: rolling the balls out on the table and shooting them off in whatever order pleases you. That's a reasonably good way to loosen up if you're about to play a match and have only a few minutes to prepare. But you should be setting time aside for *meaningful* practice emphasizing structured drills, not open play. Every great concert pianist in history had to practice scales first; he or she may not have loved it a lot, but the enhancement of fundamentals, not to mention discipline, that comes with that kind of practice is unquestionably what helped lead to greatness.

If pool is still relatively new to you—and maybe even if it isn't—a good place to start is with a simple drill that checks the straightness of your stroke. (Remember, reduced to mechanical terms, all pool *really* consists of is the ability to bring the cue forward in a straight line and hit the cue ball exactly where you've aimed.) This drill needs no object balls, just a cue, a cue ball, and one of pool's all-time great teaching aids, which is sitting right there in front of your face on the table of your choice: the spot.

All you do is this: Place the cue ball on the spot, aim it into whatever pocket you like, and fire. *Then* look at your follow-through in relation to the spot where you placed the cue ball. Does your cue point straight over its middle, or have you been caught "steering"? If you're swerving, for whatever reason, that's a habit that simply must be broken; it can't possibly help you, and does figure to hurt you. You should try this drill hitting the cue ball both in its vertical center and with sidespin. A straight stroke is an absolute must.

Players of other eras used to practice stroking into the open mouth of a Coke bottle, or through the handle on a coffee cup, without touching the sides of the opening. The same objectives would be served, I guess, but those techniques don't represent anything you can do on a pool table. It seems to me the lesson is better learned utilizing the same type of stroke you use in your game.

Obviously, the drill I've just explained isn't something you're going to want to do for very long unless you need the repetitions to get your stroke grooved. Let's proceed to some significant object-ball drills. Wisconsin's Jerry Briesath, an authentic dean among pool teachers, instructs newcomers to position play with a drill involving just two object balls rolled out on the table at random but not close together. The student selects a cue-ball location that will let him or her pocket the first ball easily *and* get the position for an equally easy shot on the second. When the student can complete the drill successfully eight-out-of-ten times, a third object ball is added to the drill, and so on, until the student is finally confronting all the balls. Each ball pocketed, Briesath estimates, represents a 50 percent improvement on the part of the student.

Some practice drills are better-known than others, and Diagram 100 illustrates one of the more familiar ones. The idea is to shoot the balls in that "L" into the same corner pocket in order, starting with the ball nearest the short rail and getting appropriate position on each ball in turn. You'll be using draw on the cue ball each time, of course, and expert players even discipline themselves to execute this drill without sending the cue ball to the bottom rail. This is an extremely difficult drill, and a run of six or seven balls in this mode is not to be sneezed at. The real key, as usual, is concentration.

Another good drill to improve your draw stroke is the circle of Diagram 101a. Start anywhere within that circle you like, and shoot any ball into any pocket—but your cue ball can't leave the circle. The challenge here comes up when you don't leave yourself anything quite as straight-in as you'd like. This drill will help you improve on stroking your draw shots and improving your cue-ball control.

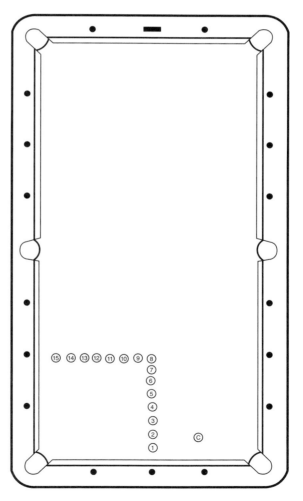

Diagram 100.

Personally, I spend more time with the drill represented in Diagram 101b than any other, although there are a number of teachers who might take issue with the way I do it. After stringing the balls across the middle of the table (I might use ten or twelve instead of all fifteen), I place the cue ball just behind the "string" (the invisible line between the far second diamonds on the long rails) for a straight-in shot on the ball nearest the rail, striving for a perfect cue-ball kill. After I make the shot, I proceed to the next shot and try to repeat it. Some players discipline themselves by beginning all over again if they miss a shot, but to me, that breeds negativity. The idea behind concentrating on a cue-ball kill is that it gets me thinking cue ball, not object ball. If I line the shot up straight and kill the cue ball properly, the object ball will automatically be in the hole. (The experts, incidentally, seem to advocate practicing straight shots where the object ball is exactly halfway between the cue ball and the pocket, so you might want to think about stringing the balls across at the third-diamond line instead of center table.) This same drill is useful for practicing cue-ball follow, then draw. Try for two or three diamonds' worth of cue-ball movement after contact at first, building up to where you can pocket balls with all the speed you're comfortable with.

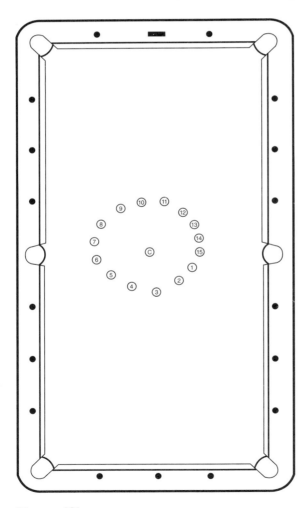

Diagram 101a.

But let's say you *still* want to roll all the balls out on the table and practice your shotmaking. There are still at least five structured approaches you can take to this kind of drill, and any and all of them will help improve your game. Make sure all the balls are separated—if two are close, that's OK, but nothing frozen—and you may also want to keep them all at least a ball's width off any rail.

1. Try shooting the balls off without allowing your cue ball to touch a second object ball after contacting the one you made.

2. Try shooting the balls off without allowing your cue ball to touch a rail after object-ball contact. Since this is considerably harder than the first, allow yourself some secondary object-ball contact if you absolutely must. Some top players believe this drill should be practiced to the exclusion of all other forms of pool for two weeks, if you're really serious about improving; that's a little parochial for me, but the drill is certainly worth trying.

3. Try shooting them off in numerical order. This is the way most Nine-Ball players practice anyway, but those extra six balls complicate things more than you'd think. Efren Reyes, the brilliant Philippine player, practices just about nothing else.

4. Try shooting off the striped balls first, then the solids (or vice versa), saving the 8 for last.

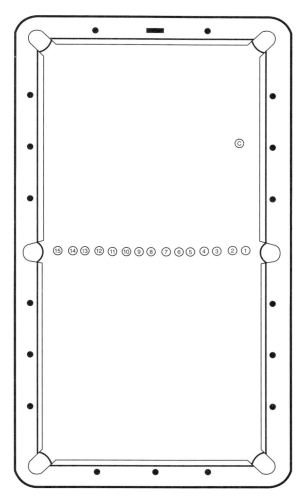

Diagram 101b.

5. Try playing solo "cribbage," that is, pocketing two consecutive balls whose values total 15 (the 1-14, 2-13, etc.), saving the 15 for last. This drill will help you learn to focus on pocketing one ball while obtaining position on a second one. This is the essence of all pool strategy—if you could do that on every shot, you'd be unbeatable.

As the old Lite Beer commercial used to say, "Practice, practice, practice." But do it so as to get the maximum out of it.

2

Advanced Eight-Ball

Just as the game of pool is underrated by those who don't know it, Eight-Ball is underrated by those who do.

Forget that it's often the first formal pool game you learn. Forget that you see it being played by kids and beginners a lot. It's really a subtle, deceptive game that, when properly played, borrows from whatever skills you have for any other pool game you know. And none of these skills counts more in Eight-Ball than what you know about Straight Pool.

If two good Eight-Ball players go head to head, the better Straight-Pool player between them should win, in the long run. There's really only one distinction: In Eight-Ball, you blast the balls open to begin the game. That fact alone makes it totally infeasible for me to take you through typical patterns; there is no such thing. What we will do is see how Straight-Pool principles might be applied to any given layout.

Eight-Ball is probably the game that introduced you to pool, even if you did call it "Stripes and Solids." It's the game around which entire leagues, which encompass hundreds of thousands of players nationally, are organized. It's the game of choice among the vast majority of those 40,000,000+ estimated to play pool once or more annually.

And almost everybody plays it incorrectly.

Despite the fact that the balls are blast-broken open to begin the game, Eight-Ball is not (or *should* not be) a game of luck. If you want to begin winning a much higher percentage of Eight-Ball games than you are now, you're going to have to embrace an unorthodox pool concept: *Pocketing balls can very easily lead to your disadvantage.*

This is not a typographical error. I know you've been focused on getting a ball into a hole ever since you were a kid; after all, that's how you get a second consecutive turn, and after you sink enough balls, you win, right?

Well, yes and no, especially in Eight-Ball. Sure, if you can run out your seven solids or stripes plus the 8 consecutively in a single turn, you win. But Eight-Ball is simply not going to present you with that many such opportunities—especially not on smaller-than-regulation-size tables that you'll find in most bars, where you have the same number of balls but 16 square feet less playing area in which to manage them. Most of the time, you'll be looking at table layouts which offer both open shots and stymies. And the critical point to be made here is this: Unless you have a sound plan for dealing with each trouble spot to free your tied-up object balls, you're slitting your own throat by sinking the balls that are already free.

One member of a repeating national champion team states the case in intriguing terms: "Think of Eight-Ball as military strategy. Each ball you make, when you *don't* run out the game, represents a dead soldier that can no longer help you in the war."

In more tranquil terms, each ball you sink represents one more ball you can't use to hide the cue ball behind and play your opponent safe. And Eight-Ball, correctly played, involves far more safety-play than you'd think.

At the same time, when you have fewer balls on the table than your opponent, it becomes far easier for *him* to play *you* safe, because he has more places to duck the cue ball. Unless your remaining balls are situated right in front of pockets, it's so much easier to avoid those table areas where he'd be leaving you anything good.

When you have more balls left than your opponent does, that's very much to your advantage—not your disadvantage. In fact, if he gets down to his last few balls (the fewer the better) and doesn't run out the game, and you have lots of balls left, you're a solid favorite to win as long as you play correctly!

Yet many Eight-Ball players will immediately commence firing at the first open balls they see. Apparently it's too tough a habit to break—or, deliberately *not* pocketing balls is too difficult a nuance to pick up. So there's a whole universe of pool players out there that you can beat by playing smarter, even if they're better shotmakers than you. We can state the case even more unequivocally than that: The only time you should go for a winning run-out in Eight-Ball is when you're absolutely certain that you will run out. (Note that I didn't say "that you *can* run out" but "that you *will* run out.") All other times, concentrate on safe leaves for your opponent. Let him shoot balls into holes, or try to, while you instead play the game as it should be played. It's not unlike a boxer versus a brawler; the boxer should win, if he doesn't make any mistakes. It will also be devastating to your opponent to come to the table repeatedly without open shots, and that's yet another edge for you. (Playing the game defensively like this, by the way, may not make you overwhelmingly popular. But did you come to win or to socialize?)

The "Tidy Up First" tactic I explained earlier in the chapter on Straight-Pool position play makes considerably less sense in the game of Eight-Ball. It may be desirable to pocket balls when you can leave your opponent completely safe or when tidying up can lead to an outright win or to locking up your opponent. Otherwise, it's far more worthwhile to leave your balls near pockets, in "Will-Call" fashion, than in them; and almost as valuable to leave your balls on rails between your opponent's ball(s) and the pockets.

Further, the only proper times to separate the clusters that have your balls tied up are when you have both a shot that will send your cue ball into the cluster *and* a safety-valve ball that you can count on shooting next no matter where those newly separated balls go. For excellent explanations on Eight-Ball strategy, I recommend the videotapes *The Art of 8 Ball* and *No Time for Negative* by expert player Jim Reid.

Let's take a look at some playing examples, starting with how you select stripes or solids. First, you and your opponent should agree on the rules beforehand, especially if you're matched up against someone you don't play regularly. There are different sets of rules regarding how the balls should be racked, what happens if you make the 8-ball on the break, what happens if you don't make the required cue-ball contact with your own balls, etc. Most of the time you'll be playing by whatever rules are commonly played in that location, usually known as "house rules." Assuming you're playing under current Billiard Congress of America rules, the most important of these rules are (1) the balls can be racked any way you choose as long as the 8-ball is in the middle and the two bottom-corner positions in the rack are occupied by one striped ball and one solid, rather than two of either; (2) sinking the 8 on the break neither wins nor loses the game outright; it simply spots up again; (3) a player is not committed to either stripes or solids until he or she sinks a ball *as intended* (i.e., balls that go in on the break don't count, even if more solids fall than stripes or vice versa; the table is still "open" until somebody makes something in the pocket he or she meant to); (4) should a player fail to contact the required striped or solid ball first with the cue ball, that player's opponent gets cue-ball-in-hand (that is, the cue ball may be placed anywhere on the table, and any legal ball is fair game).

Breaking the Balls

The Eight-Ball break looks like a brute strength, "hit and hope" proposition, but it's not. Actually, it should be a controlled stroke, with a definite beginning, middle, and end, just like any other pool stroke. (Which is *not* to say, by the way, that you should break with your regular ball-pocketing stroke; you should not.) However, you might well consider some adjustments when taking your stance, forming your bridge, and delivering. Most players spread their legs a bit wider, for instance, and lengthen their bridge by a few inches (that is, they place their bridge hand that much farther back on the cue; some also hold the cue a bit lower with their stroking hand). But what's essential is that you don't allow yourself to become excited about hitting the ball with all your might. Instead, maintain the regular rhythm of your practice strokes without rushing into the break itself.

Uncontrolled speed actually does some brutal things to your break. At the very outset of your stroke, your practice strokes lose rhythm because you're dwelling on all that force you're about to summon. Ditto your mental rehearsals; they suffer because instead of seeing and feeling control and smoothness, you're thinking power. The arc in your backswing will be tremendously exaggerated, making it much harder to keep the actual stroke level. You'll be less accurate in hitting the cue ball where you want to—dead center—and at that peak speed, your unwanted, uncontrolled English will be magnified many times after impact. You probably will be less accurate about hitting the head ball in the rack where you want to—right on the nose—as well.

That's what you're sacrificing when you just rear back and fire. What you get in return is a *possibility*—no more—that some of the object balls will roll a few feet farther, which is no guarantee that they'll fall someplace as a result. And worst of all, your cue ball is probably flying around like a balloon with its air just released, with up to 15 balls moving around simultaneously. In short, you have nothing going for you at this point but Dame Fortune to help you sink a ball and get a shot at a second one. Don't trust the lady all that often. She has this way of wetting down your chalk.

Rhythm and concentration will help you control the speed you need for the break. Hit it hard, sure, but be certain that your stroke has a beginning, middle, and end, and not the brute-strength herky-jerky lunge you see all the time. Tighten your grip on the butt *slightly*, but no more than that. Then stroke the thing smooth and pure. You'll get maximum impact as well as control if you hit the cue ball dead center; it will arrive at the stack with no natural spin of its own for the balls to absorb, and remember, with that kind of impact, any English at all would be tremendously increased.

If your stroke is level, a center-ball hit on the cue ball that sends it into the head ball dead-on (should you be breaking from dead center behind the string) will produce this effect: The albino will be rejected in the direction of the middle of the table, *and it should die there.* Don't mistake this for the force-follow effect, in which the cue ball makes contact, backs up, and then plows in again for little secondary spurts. It happens when you hit the cue ball either too high or too low; it's very dramatic to see and probably makes you think of spectacular Freudian things too, but it's still uncontrolled and dangerous. The center of the table is where your rock will be safest from all those flying missiles, and if you've stroked the break correctly, you're a favorite to make something and have the rest pretty well open. And you can make that a mighty big edge.

Where should you contact the stack? That depends on what rules you're playing by. If, for instance, you've agreed to rules that award

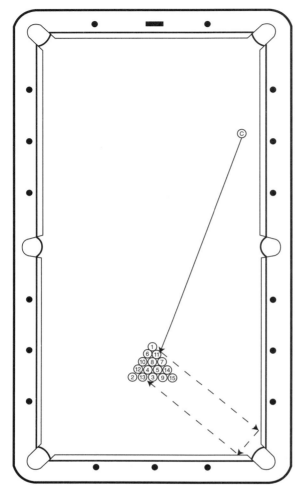

Diagram 102.

the game outright to a player sinking the 8 on the break, there is a breaking technique that could send the 8 in the direction of a side pocket (although, on balance, this remains a very low probability). This break is illustrated in Diagram 102: Place your cue ball to the side of the table (but far enough off the rail that you can bridge and stroke comfortably), and aim for the ball just behind the head ball in the rack. Use low-inside English—right-hand spin, in the diagram—and you'll actually get two whacks at the rack, one on the way in and the second coming off those two bottom rails. In theory, the 8 doesn't go far as a result of your first contact; it just hangs around waiting for the second impact to move it out. Wherever it goes, this "double whammy" approach should do a pretty efficient job of separating the clustered balls. You *must* utilize the inside English, otherwise you're unlikely to bend back to that long rail or come off the bottom rail with anywhere near the speed you want.

If you're playing that you *don't* win by sinking the 8 on the break, however, why break as though you were? What most good players will do when playing Eight-Ball or Nine-Ball (that is, games in which the balls are blast-broken open to start) is find the table's "live" areas for breaking, just as bowlers read the grooves and rolls of unfamiliar lanes. (The side of the table, as described in the previous paragraph, is a good starting place; so is the table's head spot, directly opposite that head ball you're preparing to smash.) No matter where you break from—unless you're trying the technique of Diagram 102—your objective is to pop that head ball just as full as you can, keeping your cue level and striking the cue ball in its exact center. The effect you want is for the cue ball to leap back from its initial contact and stop dead in the center of the table. This should give you the maximum number of shooting options.

Don't fall victim to too much "body English," even though competitive pressure can make it mighty hard to avoid. All that jumping and twisting around adds nothing whatsoever to your stroke and could be detrimental if you leap out of your shooting stance too early. Advanced players do have their quirks for achieving added leverage when breaking. Some plant their front legs under the table and actually brace against that contact; others push off their back legs at the point of cue-ball contact. One rising star, Minnesota's Jimmy Wetch, leans so far over the table in his stance he looks like the Tower of Pisa. But you will be satisfied with a solid stance and executing your stroke with as much cue-ball speed as you can control—no more.

Winning with Defense

It's fair to say that the majority of competitive pool played today is on a smaller-than-regulation-size table. That's because of the advent of tavern pool leagues (the American Poolplayers' Association alone consists of hundreds of thousands of players and requires a full-time staff in St. Louis to administrate). So what happens to the game of Eight-Ball, as we've considered it, when the playing area shrinks from a 40½-square-foot table to a 32-square-foot table or, even more commonly, a 24½-square-foot table? You don't have as much room to move the cue ball around and that means far fewer run-out opportunities.

And yet, there's a winning strategy that's just as certain. Instead of beating your head against the wall trying to negotiate all those packed-together balls, use them to your advantage.

Diagram 103, for instance, shows you a game that *might* be winnable, playing the solids, but it would take a real player to execute this run-out. The 4-ball in that far corner pocket is where it begins; the keys are in getting position from the 1 to the 2—either in the corner or the side—and then from the 2 to the 3. The winning sequence I see here is 4-1-2-3-7-5-6-8.

Yet the problem with that sequence is that, once begun, you've committed yourself to running out the game. If you miss anywhere along the way, or misplay your position, you've just killed off valu-

able soldiers and are probably a favorite to lose, the precise mistake
that the lion's share of Eight-Ball players blunder into. So why not
simply drive the 5 out of there, and park your cue ball under the 6
and 13? It's easy; it leaves your opponent nothing; and probably
best of all, he's likely not used to responding to 8-ball safeties.
That means he must take on a whole new mind-set for this decid-
edly mental game, which is no easy psychological task. Each time
you leave your opponent nothing to shoot, you send him into a
nasty little self-struggle wondering if he is being outsmarted.

   Diagram 104 shows you a far more typical 8-ball leave off the
break: Some balls open (specifically, the 9 and 11; should you elect
solids, you *might* even make that tough 1-3 combination and get

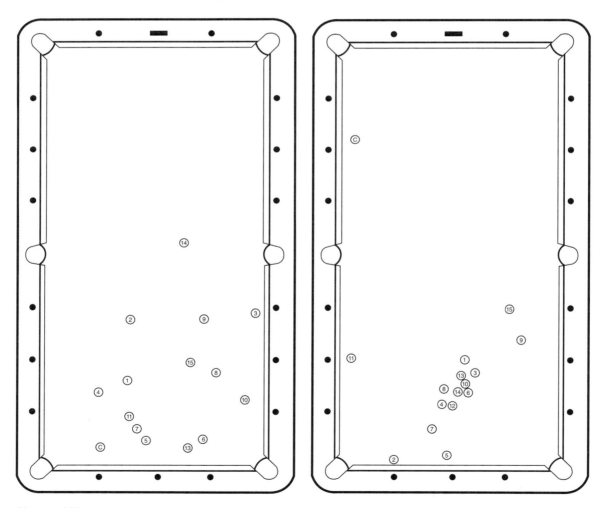

Diagram 103.   **Diagram 104.**

position for one of the three solids near the bottom rail) and some still clustered. But why bother with those open shots, when whatever is to follow is so totally uncertain? Far wiser to slap the 15 off the outside of the 9, driving both out of play, and draw the cue ball back to the end rail. Let your opponent figure out what to do with the mess. Yes, you've surrendered the table, and your opponent could theoretically win without giving you another turn. But he or she could also win the lottery, too, nearly as much of a long shot as what you've left him or her.

Diagram 105 represents the most fertile defensive-play scenario of all: Not only do you leave your opponent nothing, but you put him or her in genuine trouble. Make the 7; then deliberately miss the 2, leaving it smack in front of that opposite-corner pocket and leaving the cue ball up against the 10 and 14. (I probably shouldn't be telling you this, but a savvy hustler would also put on a modest act of chagrin after missing the 2.) Your opponent has hardly any safety

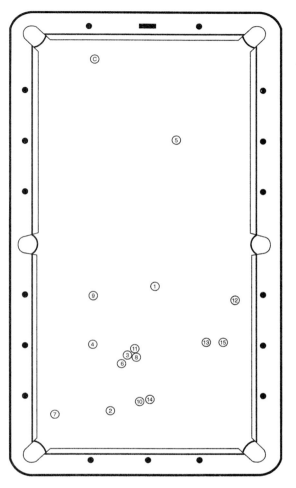

Diagram 105.

whatsoever, while you're poised to proceed, depending on where you're left, with either the 2 or 4 (the latter could be a break shot, too). (The reason we don't begin our plan with the 5 is that it's too tough and, equally important, you might not get position on the 7 next; in either case, your opponent can get the edge on you if he knows what he's doing.)

Anytime you decide to take on a cluster in Eight-Ball, a safety-valve shot is an absolute must—and the number of balls available to take on that role is necessarily smaller, because only half of the total balls are legally yours to begin with. Expert Eight-Ball players will also advise you to make the safety-valve shot one directly opposite the ball you just sank, eliminating the gamble of your break shot.

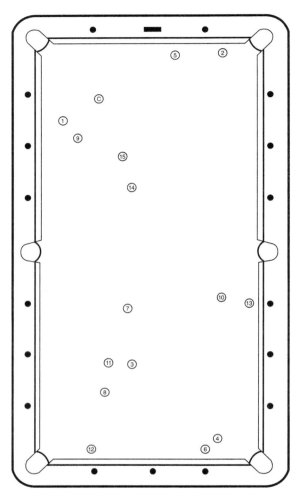

Diagram 106.

Playing the Game

To begin with, let's assume that in this and all the other forms of Eight-Ball we'll discuss, you and your opponent have agreed to "play honest"; that is, each player must try to hit his own ball before making contact with any other.

Now let's play our way through two racks, one relatively simple, the next somewhat more challenging.

Diagram 106 shows you the balls well broken but nothing made. It's your shot, and your choice of stripes or solids, too. Which do you begin with?

Neither. What you do before you do anything else in Eight-Ball is to check out the 8-ball. Is it an A-, B-, or C-ball (since you're obviously not going to use it as a D)? In Diagram 106, the 8-ball is an A, available to the nearest corner pocket.

Now is when you begin to choose between the stripes and solids, and the right way to do that is not necessarily to pick out the simplest shot immediately available. What you look for now is which set of balls offers the most logical path to the 8-ball, just as the balls lie? All the balls in the diagram seem to be A's, except for the 5, and that's part of a simple combination shot.

A good player could run out this game by choosing either stripes or solids in this case, but I think that same good player would be much more likely to choose stripes. The reasons are these: Although the solids offer three quite easy shots in the head corner pockets (5-2, 5, and 1), position on the 1 will be somewhat tricky; so will transitional plays from the head of the table to the foot, for the remaining solid balls; and most importantly, the 11 and 12 balls offer a more natural key-shot sequence to get to the 8, and the striped balls lie so as to lead the player right down the table with minimum effort.

So you begin with the 9, instead of that big fat 5-2 combination. The 9 is actually only slightly harder than that anyway. Roll it down the table and hold your cue ball there for a side-pocket shot at the 15 (Diagram 107). Do the same with your cue ball for the 14 (Diagram 108), and follow for the 10 and 13 (Diagrams 109 and 110). Follow a foot or so for a negotiable angle on the 12 (Diagram 111), and play position using one rail, not two, for the 11 in the side (Diagram 112), which leaves you ready to pop Othello into the subway via the corner (Diagram 113). All you did there was play good Straight Pool: You used the rails only as strictly needed, you never touched a secondary object

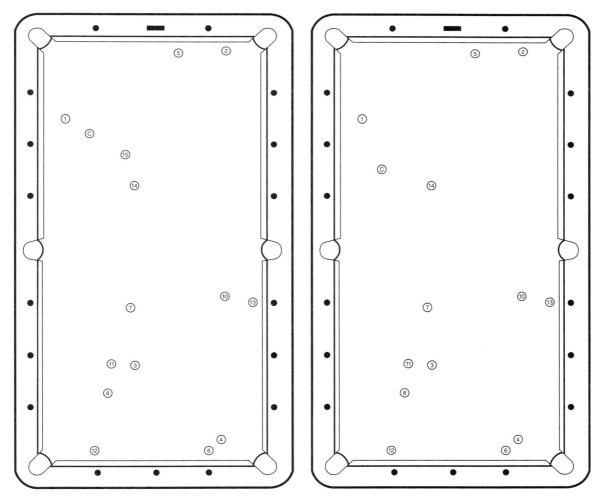

Diagram 107. **Diagram 108.**

ball, and your sequence was nothing more than seven cornermosts in a row. You can see that by reexamining Diagram 106.

Let's try something a little tougher. In Diagram 114, you have more than mere A-balls to consider. The 8-ball is definitely a C. If you went with the solids here, even though the 5 is a cinch in the side, you'd have to contend with two B-balls, the 1 and 6, and a C, the 3. And you don't have a really good D-ball.

If you take the stripes, you still get a C, the 10. But you can move it with the 12-ball, a good D-ball that you can play position for whenever you wish and may even be able to play with a safety valve behind it.

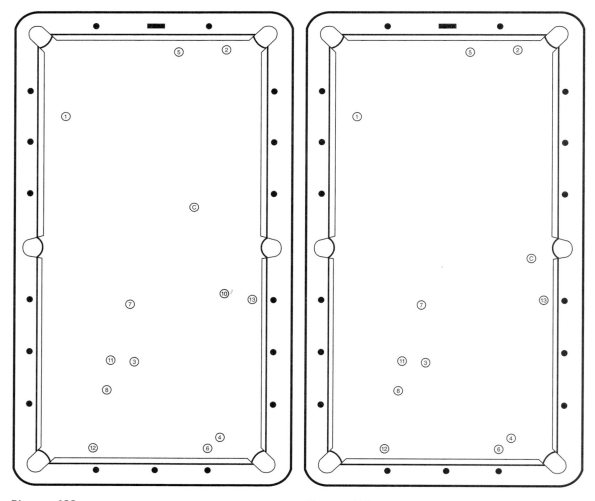

Diagram 109.   **Diagram 110.**

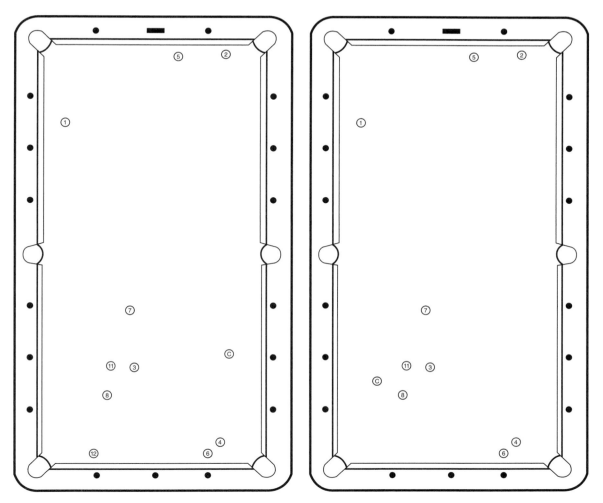

Diagram 111.   **Diagram 112.**

So take stripes. Both a solid and a stripe fell on the break, and you can get out here by playing six cornermosts in succession: the 14 (gone in Diagram 115), the 15 (gone in Diagram 116) with enough follow for an angle on the 13, the 13 (gone in Diagram 117) with enough follow for an angle on the 12, the 12 (gone in Diagram 118) softly enough that the 11 acts as a safety valve. In Diagram 118, the balls are now open enough for you to win, shooting the 11 in the side (Diagram 119), then the 10 in the corner (Diagram 120), then the 8 in the opposite corner.

I have not deliberately oversimplified these racks. The fact is, Eight-Ball can be won from the break, assuming that the break leaves you

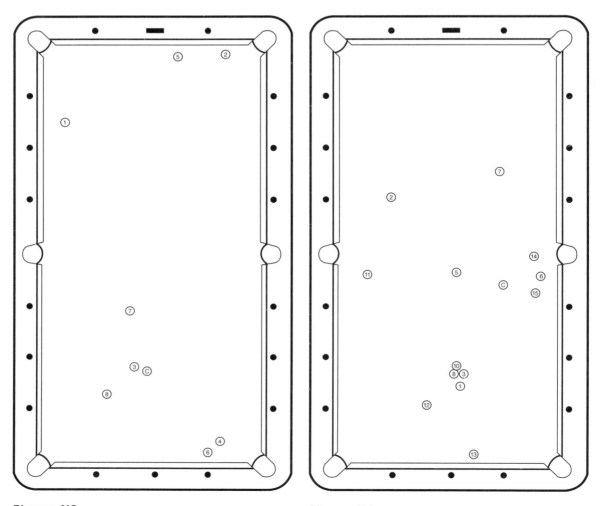

Diagram 113.   **Diagram 114.**

something to shoot at. It's not that hard to break the balls apart; that depends as much upon a smooth level stroke as it does on brute strength. And following the break, you generally can put a game plan together, despite the fact that there are all those balls all over the table. Where the game gets tied up in knots, more often than not, is *after* the balls are broken, by the players' incorrect shot selection and/or failure to execute their plans. Because the game begins with a freewheeling break, the temptation is there to keep clobbering the balls willy-nilly all game. But don't do that. Give this game the precision it deserves, and it will reward you.

What you learn here hopefully will keep you from making too many mistakes, but it won't keep you from missing. I want you to learn to think your way through each new situation confronting you, each time you come to the table. Misses are part of the game; the guy you're playing will miss shots, too. And whichever of you is better at *recouping* his misses will win. Generally speaking, there should be *some* plan available to you that will advance your cause, even if it's nothing more than leaving him the toughest shots possible. And if he does trap you sufficiently that you can't win the game, then he deserves the win him-

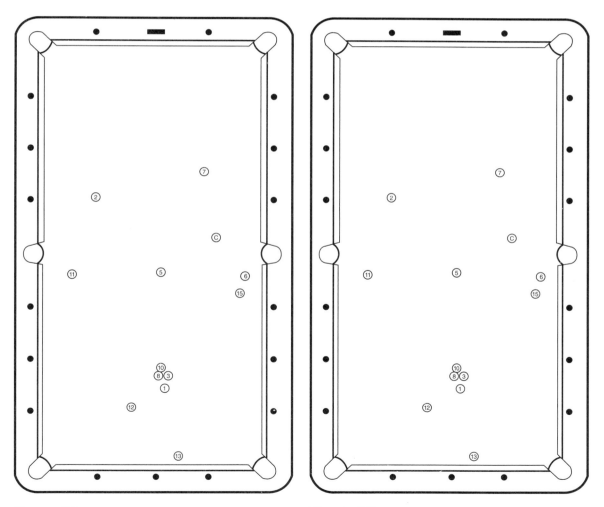

Diagram 115.   **Diagram 116.**

self. There's always the next game. Don't give up, and above all, never stop thinking.

Put the object ball in the subway and put the cue ball someplace beneficial. That's all that every form of pool known to man comes down to. Nobody can do that every time, of course. But you'll be surprised how your chances of accomplishing correct moves increase as long as you keep thinking about what those moves might be.

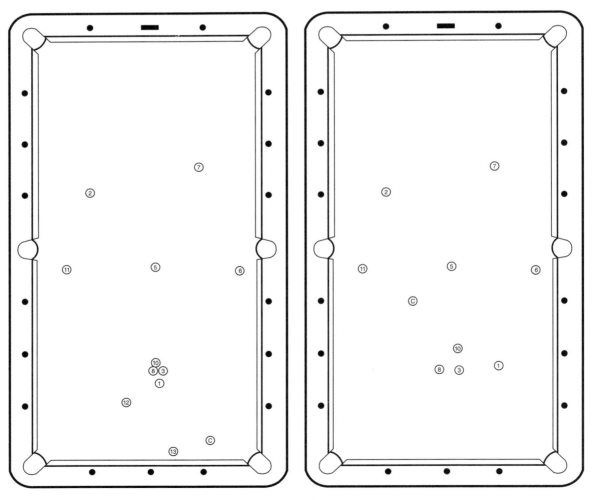

Diagram 117.   **Diagram 118.**

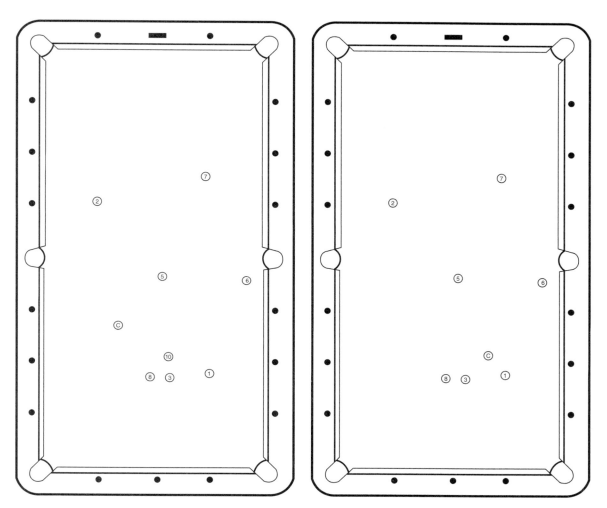

Diagram 119.   **Diagram 120.**

Last-Pocket Eight-Ball

Here's an advanced form of the game that makes even greater use of
your Straight-Pool skills. In this game, you must sink the 8-ball in
the same pocket in which you made your final object ball, whether it
was a stripe or a solid.

On the surface, it would seem that all you need to modify in your
thinking is the relationship between the 8-ball and your last ball pre-
ceding it. Instead of establishing that your last ball will lead you to an
open shot on the 8, you must establish a two-ball but one-pocket relationship between them. Choose a plan that will win for you, rather

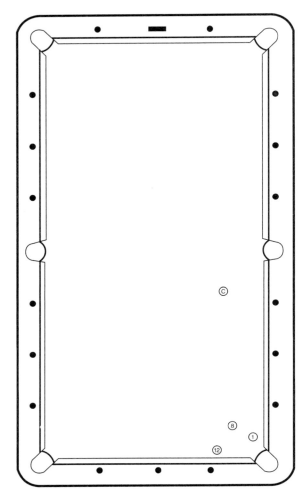

Diagram 121.

than one that first lets you pocket all your object balls and then lets you tend to the matter of the 8.

This seems self-explanatory, but Last-Pocket is a deceptive game for that very reason. Once you're ready for your last object ball, and hopefully the 8 after that, you're actually quite vulnerable. Now I don't want you to create any fear of the situation in which you address the last two balls of the game; after all, it means that you've got first crack at winning the game outright. But I do want you to understand that should you miss that last ball—or worse, make the last ball but miss the 8—you're really not even a favorite to win the game any more.

The reason for that is that your opponent would then have an unmistakable picture of what it takes to leave you safe. He can arrange his entire remaining sequence around that; he may even legally abandon that sequence in favor of driving the 8-ball someplace where it's no longer compatible with the last object ball for the pocket you intended.

Diagram 121 shows you what I mean. If you had just missed that 1-ball and left me nothing I liked from among my remaining stripes, you can be sure that I'd move that 8-ball up to the other end of the table. The most you could expect then would be a tough bank shot on the 8, once you pocketed your 1 where you originally missed it. In the diagram, note that I could move the 8 either with one of my own object balls, or I could use the cue ball directly; and naturally, I'd take appropriate cautionary measures to be sure that I didn't accidentally sink the 8 someplace, which would cost me the game. So even though you *appear* to have the upper hand in the game of Diagram 121, it isn't necessarily that way at all.

It's even worse to make your last object ball and then miss the 8. Unless you leave it *very* close to the pocket where you aimed it, leaving you without a second opportunity is quite a simple matter; it requires only reasonable thinking and care on your opponent's part.

And whatever else you do, do *not* formulate a sequence that saves your last object ball and the 8-ball for a side pocket (unless both balls represent absolutely cinch shots that you can be 100 percent sure of making the first time). If you make your last object ball in a side (or if your opponent manages to make it there for you legally, a smart but rare move) and then fail to make the 8, a blind man could play you safe for the rest of the game. Which, of course, gets back to your vulnerability once those last two balls are left.

If the shoe is on the other foot, and it's your opponent who has failed to get out, your first priority should be defense rather than offense. Try to win the game yourself, sure, but choose patterns that shut your opponent out in the event of a miss. Most Last-Pocket games allow you and your opponent to go for the same pocket if you both happen to sink your last object balls there; in that case, it becomes increasingly tougher to play your opponent safe, since you're trying for precisely the same kind of position. So choose shots that you can be sure of.

That situation produces some of the longest Last-Pocket games, simply because each player is afraid to leave his opponent anything. So the two bunt the 8-ball around defensively; or if either player does get a shot, he'll probably hit it with some extra speed to make sure the thing doesn't stick around if it misses. Another long defensive struggle situation occurs where one player is going for a corner at the foot of the table and his opponent wants the opposite corner pocket at the head of the table. The game then becomes something like One-Pocket with the table turned sideways, and in that case I think you'll see a lot more games that are not won by one player as much as they are lost by the other.

Alabama Eight-Ball

In this game, the player shooting the solid balls is required to make his 1-ball into a side pocket, and his opponent must pocket his 15-ball in the opposite side pocket. The players may agree before the game as to which side pocket gets which ball, or they may simply play first-come, first-serve, with the player who pockets his side-pocket ball last being required to take the side pocket in which his opponent did not score. If the 1 or 15 is pocketed anywhere else, it is respotted at once and the shooter's inning ends.

Again, this game favors the better Straight-Pool player. Making your ball in the side pocket first makes you a considerable favorite to win the game, and you should plan a sequence that lets you do that as early as you possibly can. The longer you let it go, the fewer object balls you have available to lead you logically to a side-pocket shot. And as before, saving your side-pocket shot for last is absolutely suicidal.

In fact, if your opponent gets his 1 or 15 out near a side pocket, you should immediately begin looking for moves that will clear that ball out of there, even if it means passing up a chance to score yourself. Presumably, you're playing by rules that prohibit you from shooting directly at your opponent's ball; but you can use your own object balls to accomplish the same thing, and naturally your opportunities for such a move are at their greatest early in the game, when most of your object balls are still available.

Even though shots are available to me in Diagram 122, I'd be much wiser to play one of my object balls into my opponent's 15 and drive it where it can't be pocketed in the side. My 1-ball is not readily available for pocketing in the side, or else I'd choose a more aggressive sequence. But in the layout you see, my opponent definitely has the edge, and I want to take that edge away.

In racking the balls for Alabama, incidentally, the 1 and 15 balls should occupy the slots immediately behind the 8-ball.

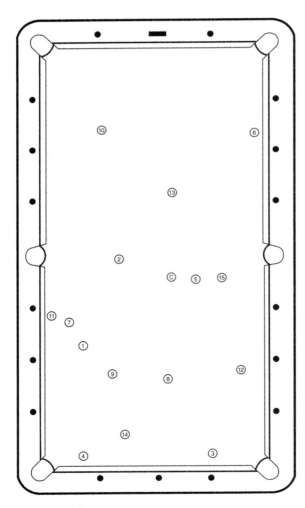

Diagram 122.

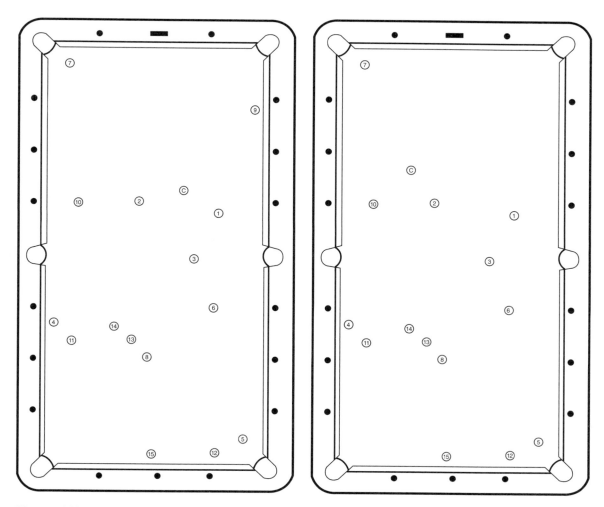

Diagram 123.

Diagram 124.

Two for You to Solve

Just as we did in Straight Pool, let's see how you would think your way through these two racks of Eight-Ball. In each case, you have your choice of stripes or solids; and just for an extra tad of discipline, assume that in the second set of diagrams, the game is Last-Pocket, too. My solutions follow the diagrams.

Diagram 123 might have fooled you somewhat. If you chose the solids, you'd have your choice of four very easy shots to begin with (the 1, 2, 5, and 7); and indeed, a competent player could win this game outright shooting either stripes or solids. I chose stripes here,

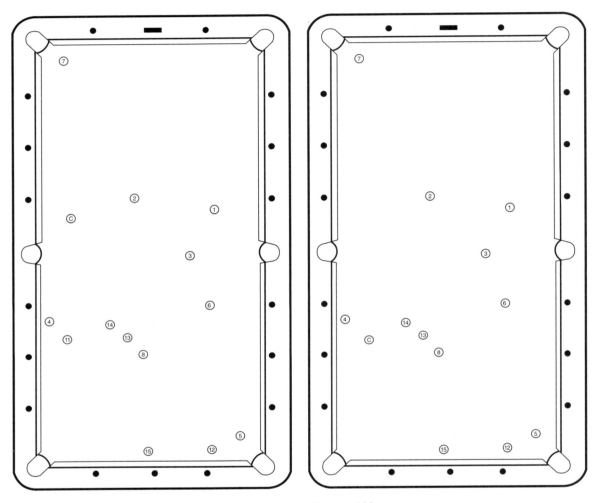

Diagram 125.   **Diagram 126.**

even though my opening shot, the 9-ball, is slightly tougher than any of those solids. Still, once the 9 is gone, the rest of the stripes arrange themselves in a quite logical sequence, and in my opinion, the 15 and 12 offer better keys to the 8-ball than any combination of solids. As Diagrams 124 through 130 show you, the winning sequence (after the 9-ball) is 10-11-14-13-15-12-8 in the corner.

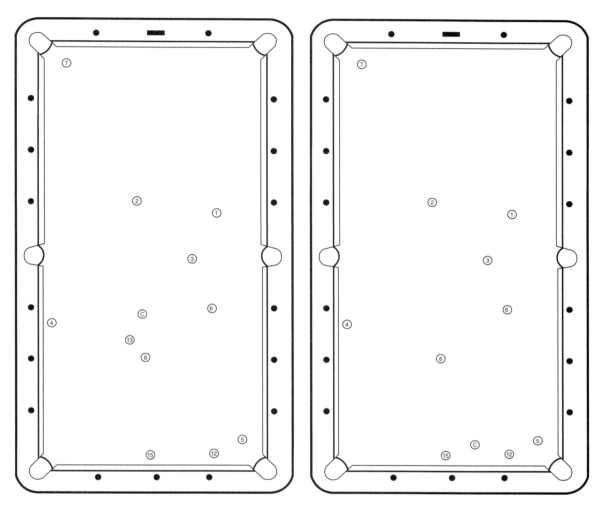

Diagram 127. **Diagram 128.**

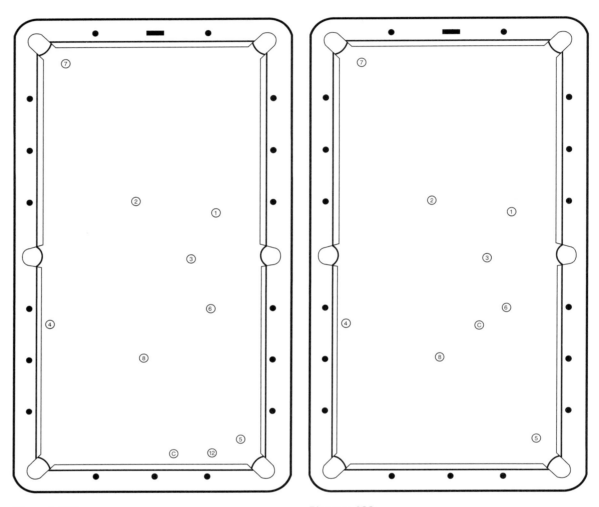

Diagram 129.   **Diagram 130.**

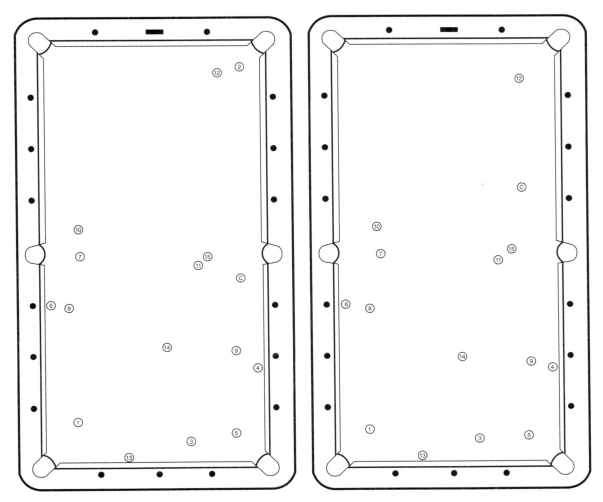

Diagram 131.

Diagram 132.

Similarly, Diagram 131 shows you two easy shots on striped balls (the 15 and 10) to get you started. But solids offer a better long-range proposition, especially for Last-Pocket. I'd get those long shots out of the way first (the 2 and 4 balls, Diagrams 132 and 133), and the rest is really pretty smooth sailing. The complete sequence, Diagrams 132 through 138, is 2-4-5-1-3-7-6-8 in the same corner as the 6. Again, any other progression you saw that would work, in either of these two racks, is just as valid as mine.

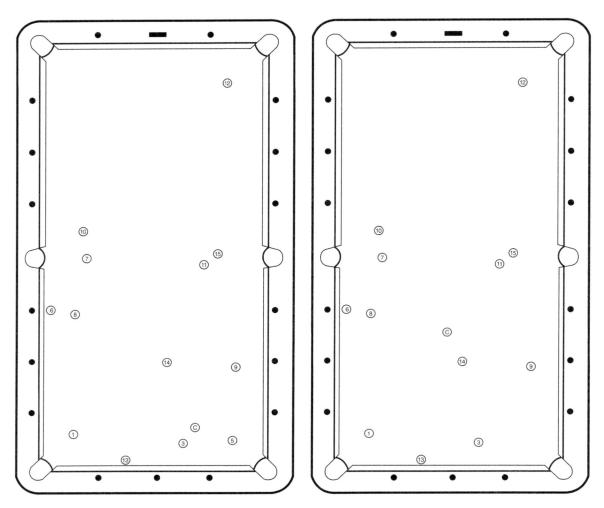

Diagram 133.   **Diagram 134.**

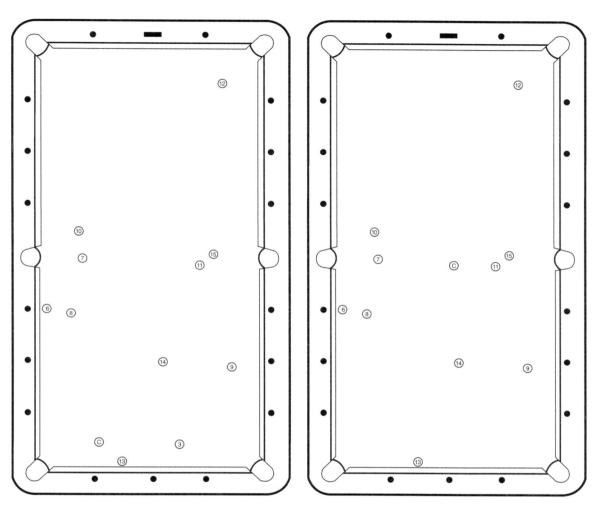

Diagram 135.

Diagram 136.

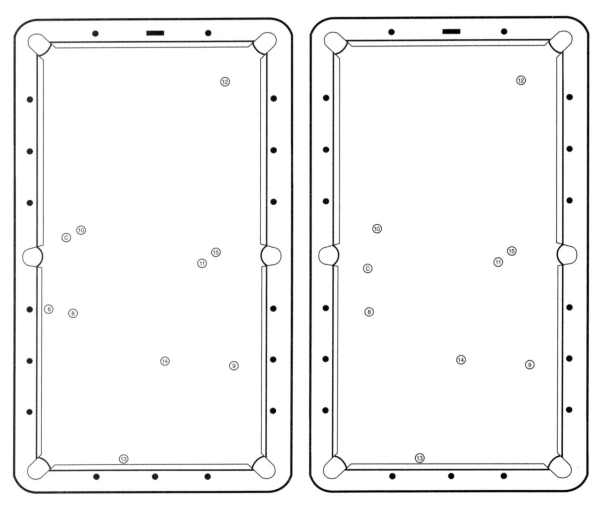

Diagram 137.   **Diagram 138.**

3

Advanced Nine-Ball

Nine-Ball is a shotmaker's delight.

To be sure, there is a certain finesse to the game, especially when two good players get together; you'll see safeties, snookers or "hooks," spectacular jump shots, and especially carom shots. But it's still basically a game of shotmaking. That's why kids take to the game so well. They're able to both pocket the ball and move their cue ball all over the table; successful Nine-Ball is little more than a combination of these two abilities.

The game has pressure all its own, too. With the exception of tournament play, and because of its speed and orientation to offense, Nine-Ball lends itself well to television and therefore is the staple of professional tournaments. The game is just about senseless unless you're playing for stakes. The game can be unpredictable, too. You'll find an uncommon number of players who can clear the first eight balls with consummate genius and then have trouble dropping the 9 into the Grand Canyon. It's quite possible that Nine-Ball is the only game where a player can do the majority of scoring and *still* lose.

Since the game begins with a free break as Eight-Ball does, there is no such thing as a typical pattern. Nine-Ball demands that your cue ball do some traveling, far more than in other pool games. And

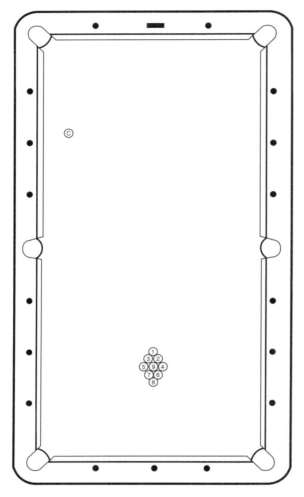

Diagram 139.

the A-B-C-D object ball categories won't work, because you don't have a choice; your shot sequence must begin with the cue ball contacting the lowest numbered ball.

The Break

The break shot is done precisely as it's done in Eight-Ball. Find a location near the long rail, allowing enough room off that rail to bridge comfortably. Find the "live" break spots with the same trial-and-error process detailed earlier and strive to hit the head ball—always the 1-ball—right on the nose. But the break in Nine-Ball can give you a more formidable advantage than in Eight-Ball, something to remember when making the break a part of any handicapped-game proposition.

Equally as important as knowledge of how and where to drive the cue ball is understanding the potential results. Let's analyze the Nine-Ball rack more closely. As you probably know by now, the balls are racked as in Diagram 139—a diamond-like shape with the 9 in the middle and the 1 up front.

Suppose you're breaking from the right. The 1-ball will travel to the left with slow to moderate speed, its exact path determined by where the cue ball hits it. If hit toward its center, it will move in the direction of the bottom-corner pocket; if hit more on the right side, it will move more toward the bottom-side pocket, precisely what many expert players will try to achieve. So, the 1 actually can be pocketed in one of three pockets, the two just mentioned plus the top-corner pocket, where it not infrequently can be banked.

The two balls directly behind the 1 rarely go far. Assuming again that the cue ball approaches from the right, the 2 will travel to the left and somewhat back; occasionally it will bank into the opposite-side pocket. Otherwise it tends to stay in the middle of the table, unless another ball kicks it away. The 3 travels weakly to the right, either sideways or forward, but because of its slow speed tends to remain in the top-right part of the table unless kicked away.

The two balls flanking the 9 are the fastest leaving the rack, the ball in the 4-ball's position moving somewhat faster than the ball racked where the 5 is on a right-sided break. However, the 4-ball will rarely fall in that near-corner pocket, while the 5 frequently does visit its corner pocket. Most often, both balls will strike the nearest long rails and continue to move.

The 9 is probably the least predictable ball in the rack. It generally travels forward and slowly, occasionally reaching the corner pocket opposite the side from which the balls are broken, but rarely reaching the corner pocket on the same side. When the 9 is pocketed on the break—and even the best players can't count on that happening more than one-out-of-ten times—it's often kicked in by another ball.

The two balls immediately behind the 9—the 6 and 7 in the diagram—aren't much better travelers than the two balls behind the 1. The 6 usually moves weakly forward and to the left, often remaining near the top rail and the left side unless kicked by another ball. It won't pocket either, unless kicked. The 7 generally moves forward and to the right with moderate speed, and once in a while, it can be sunk in the near-side pocket.

The tail ball in the rack (the 8-ball in the diagram) is the third-fastest ball leaving the rack. It will probably bank off the near short rail, and it could travel all the way down-table to score in a corner pocket. The farther on the right the 1 is struck the more the last ball will travel to the right.

The ball racked where you see the 5 is the most commonly pocketed ball when breaking from the right. The second most frequently pocketed shot on the break is the 1, pocketed in the side opposite the break side. This shot is the only shot where the player has control over the outcome. The third most likely ball to fall will be the back ball, which can bank into the corner nearest where the cue ball began.

The majority of balls that fall on the break go directly into pockets, as just described. The other shots made on the break are due to collisions between object balls, most often involving the fastest moving balls (to either side of the 9, and at the rear of the rack). But those are lucky collisions, depending on minute differences in timing and pathways, and are almost totally unpredictable.

Leave the cue ball in the middle of the table after the break as you do in Eight-Ball; this increases the chances of having a shot at the 1. This alone can affect the way a Nine-Ball game is handicapped, or even played. Suppose it's your opponent's break, and you want to make his or her transition from the 1-ball to the 2 as difficult as you can. You can achieve this by racking the 2 where you see the 6 in Diagram 139. If you're spotting your opponent another money ball, such as the 8, rack that ball where you now see the 3 or 6; those are the safest positions. If he or she changes break sides, the safest positions become those where you now see the 2 or 7.

So much for the racking of the balls. The most important advice I can give you concerning the striking of the cue ball is to utilize all the speed you can *control*, rather than all you can produce. In an ideal break, just as in Eight-Ball, your cue ball should limp back to the center of the table and die gracefully there.

Playing the Game

Nine-Ball has undergone significant rule changes since it became the pros' game of choice. Prior to TV, if a player failed to contact the lowest numbered ball first, his or her opponent had the option of playing the shot as it lay, or ordering his or her opponent to shoot again. After a second miss, the incoming player was permitted to place the cue ball anywhere he or she wished. This frequently resulted in a player's rolling the cue ball someplace without making any attempt to hit the correct ball if he didn't like the original shot, confident he or she could at least hit the required ball on the second try. This was called the "rollout rule," and what it essentially did was provide for fair play and prevent the player who failed to make a legal hit from gaining any advantage from his error. And when good Nine-Ball players got it on, rollouts were an instrument of strategy as well as justice.

Today, rollouts are all but obsolete. The only time during the game that a player may opt to roll out is immediately following the break. At any other time during a rack of Nine-Ball, failure to hit the lowest numbered ball means that the opponent gets cue-ball-in-hand immediately; three consecutive such failures constitutes automatic loss of the game.

Running nine balls in rotation is not wildly difficult to do, and when good players are in action, Nine-Ball is frequently won right from the break. This is more a function of the players' skills than it is testimony that Nine-Ball is an easy game. It is not. In the random breaking of the balls, stymies to running out the complete game will occur a lot more often than you think. When two intermediate players compete at Nine-Ball, the remaining balls after the break probably create sequencing problems at least half the time. Those problems take the form of multiple balls along the same rail, miniclusters, or balls blocking the paths of other balls to logical pockets so that what you have are long, highly improbable combination shots.

Not even the best players can transform these problems to run-out opportunities all the time. But once the balls are broken, you'll almost never see a good player choose to blast away, trusting his luck. Instead, he or she will choose to play strategy, and so should you.

First let's examine some open racks, in which the balls are pocketable in rotation as they lie (sometimes cynically called "road maps" by expert players). Later on, we'll take a look at some of the more common problems. Keep in mind that I'm still advocating using the minimum amount of force necessary to get the job done, as well as w. p.'s. But Nine-Ball requires added force on a majority of shots and offers mandatory sequences that will frequently make most, if not all, your "Whenever Possibles" impossible.

Diagram 140 shows exactly what to look for after the break: an open pocket for every object ball and plenty of space between them to work with. This rack should be run out. Try to achieve a cue-ball location on the 2 which will permit you to avoid the 6 and 9 (w. p. 3, remember?). You should probably play position on the 4 in that back-corner pocket nearest the 7 and 8, because that's the simplest shot coming off the 3. Draw the cue ball back from the 4 only as far as the line between the second diamonds on the long rails for efficient position on the 5.

The layout of Diagram 141 is even easier than that. The only problem—a modest one—is that the 3 won't clear the 6, so in playing the 1, leave an angle on the 2 to shoot the 3 into the same pocket. Again, in playing the 4, don't draw the cue ball all the way back to the rail hosting the 5 and 6; leave it anywhere in the vicinity of the 3.

Naturally, these simple analyses should be made immediately after the break. In playing ball-to-ball position, however, planning for Nine-Ball is quite different from planning for Straight Pool or Eight-Ball, as you might expect given that you must go in numerical order.

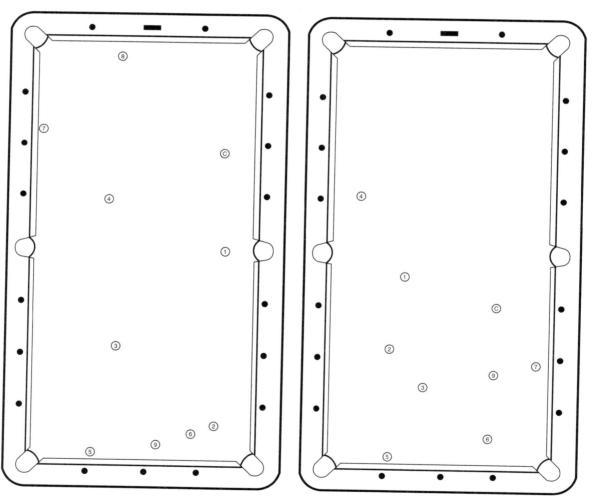

Diagram 140.   Diagram 141.

Nine-Ball Position

When you create a shot offering an angle between cue ball, object ball, and pocket—as opposed to one offering a straight line—you've prepared yourself, at least theoretically, to deliver the cue ball just about anywhere on the table. And nowhere is that more important than in Nine-Ball, where the balls are scattered at random and the layouts, most of the time, will require you to move your cue ball all over the table.

Expert Straight-Pool players plan up to six shots ahead; the best Eight-Ball players, when they decide to try for a run-out from the break, will plan a run-out eight shots ahead, or however many shots are required. In Nine-Ball, that number generally drops to three.

Here is what all-time leading tournament and money winner Mike Sigel does first when planning his Nine-Ball position: He divides the table into quadrants. He then decides how to deliver as many balls to the nearest pockets in their quadrants as the pattern will permit (which it won't always). Obviously, common sense applies; an object ball on or near the rail at the third diamond cannot be played in the near-side pocket, for instance.

He then proceeds by asking the following questions before each shot:

1. What is the next ball I want to pocket, after I pocket the one I'm shooting now?
2. Where is the most advantageous position for the cue ball to land for my next shot? How do I get there?
3. What ball(s) are going to interfere with my path (if any do), and what adjustments am I going to make as a result?

In Diagrams 140 and 141, there is no need to ask or answer question 3, but simple racks are rare. Both offer you no-brainer opportunities to get from the 1 to the 2. Additionally, both diagrams show that where you want to be on the 2 to get somewhere good on the 3 is probably on the center-table side of it, so that nearest long rail becomes your true buddy in playing position. Take a minute or two right now to think your way through these two racks following the principles outlined above. Most of the time it will not be this easy, but you've got to start someplace; and it would be lunacy to try and teach yourself this

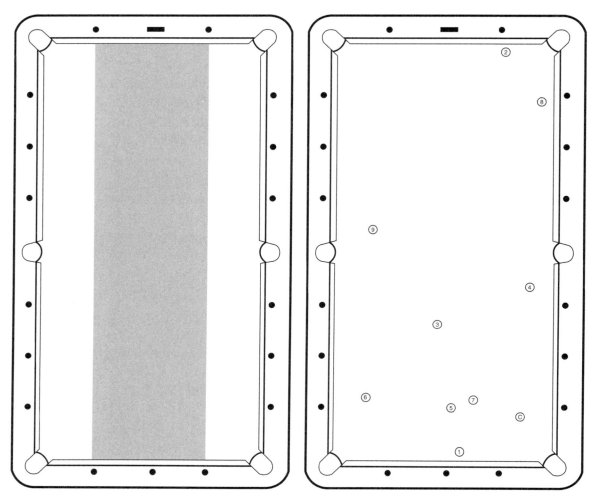

Diagram 142.   Diagram 143.

thinking process by starting with tougher racks. Your improvement will be much quicker than you think.

Diagram 142 shows you another unique position-play perspective, this one from one of the best Nine-Ball players ever, the great Buddy Hall. He visualizes the area of the table between the outside diamonds and the short rails and does everything he can to keep his cue ball in that area. This is his way of ensuring that he'll have an angle on each ball plus ample room to bridge and stroke comfortably. Hall will only permit his cue ball to stray outside the center area when he's on the 9 and wouldn't mind something straight-in for game ball.

Now let's consider a challenging layout. In Diagram 143, an analysis should determine that the upper-right table quadrant is the place to be in order to pocket the 2 in the nearest corner. The Straight-Pool lesson, "Whenever possible, use one rail instead of two or three," won't do you a bit of good here; the 5 and 7 are directly in your path. Instead, hit the 1 with left-hand draw, and use the bottom and side rails, in that order, to achieve position on the 2. (Many top players will opt for this position ploy even if they don't have to, provided the object ball is no more than one ball's width removed from that bottom rail.) Once there, make a decision about how to pocket the 2, avoid the 8, and get to the 3. The rest of the layout should be easy.

Clearly there aren't enough trees in the universe to provide the paper I'd need to cover all possible Nine-Ball problems. But you should address them all in the terms I've described—and when you encounter a layout for which there are no apparent solutions, abandon those happy thoughts about running out the game and start thinking about what else you can do that will help you win.

Nine-Ball Defense

With the advent of the one-foul-means-cue-ball-in-hand rule, defensive play becomes more important than ever in Nine-Ball, even though the game seems to be almost totally geared toward offensive play. When good players are in combat, either one is obviously an odds-on favorite to run out any game in which he or she manuevers the opponent into missing the lowest numbered ball and is then awarded cue-ball-in-hand.

Accordingly, you should abandon that delicious fantasy you have about running out the game each time you come to the table (don't be embarrassed that I know your secret; almost every player carries the same dream in his or her heart of hearts). You win nothing extra for doing so, and the game you win by outsmarting your opponent over multiple innings at the table instead of running out in one may even do you more good; it induces frustration that could well force your opponent off his or her game.

Consider Diagram 144, for instance. You might or might not sink the 1; you might or might not get past the 4 even if you do make the 1; you might or might not land somewhere juicy for the 2. That's too many contingencies for my taste. So why not simply drive the 1 out of there and back down-table, parking your cue ball behind either the

4 or 7? (Balls on or near a long rail, reasonably close to a corner pocket like this, should always be considered for snookering opportunities.)

In Diagram 145, you've made two balls on the break, have an easy shot on the 1, and separated the rest of the balls. And you *still* don't have a good run-out. The 2-6 and 3-9 combinations are for suckers only; the balls are too far apart, and each ball to be pocketed is too far from each pocket. The 1-ball is a thin cut and cue-ball control may be tricky in order to get to the 2. Then how to proceed to the 3? Bank the 1 and draw back behind the 4 and 5 instead, achieving ball-in-hand for the 1. That's *got* to be easier than what you have now.

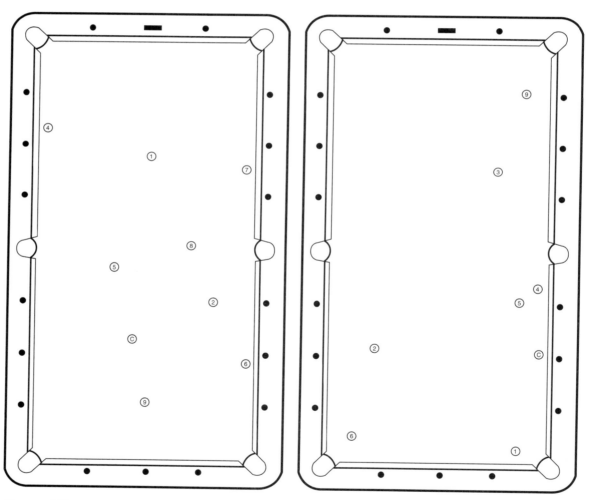

Diagram 144.   **Diagram 145.**

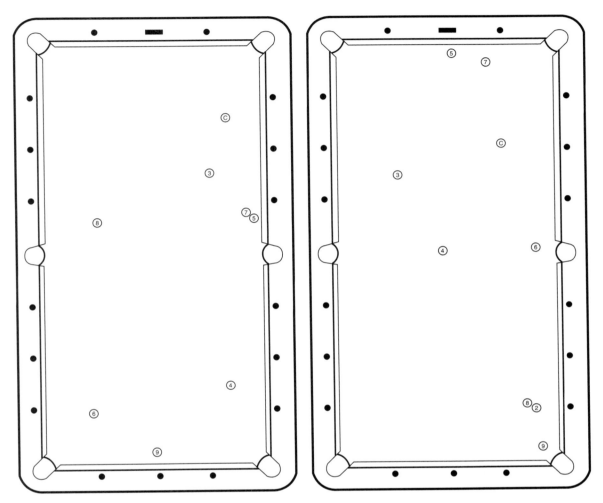

Diagram 146.   **Diagram 147.**

In Diagram 146, there's no open pocket for the 3. Even if there were, what can be done about that sticky 5-7 tangle on the near rail? Drive the 3 down-table and into the interfering 6. At the same time, nudge the 5 and 7 apart, with your cue ball. Now your opponent's got a real problem. If he or she doesn't overcome your snooker, you're a threat to run out the game; there's nothing left to stymie you. Shots like this, which combine defense with a measure of offense, are a valuable weapon in your arsenal. Train yourself to make them. The objective of correct defensive play in Nine-Ball is not simply to stop your opponent but to directly enhance your chances of winning.

Diagram 147 illustrates how Nine-Ball can toy with you. You broke almost perfectly, made the 1 in the side, and could have had a simple 2-9 combination for a quick win. Then the 8 rolled in. What now? Clip the visible edge of the 2 and try for the 9 coming off the side rail. It's odds-against, and you might even scratch, but anything's better than leaving the 9 where it is. (If the 9 weren't where it is, you might try driving the 2 out of there and killing the cue ball for a snooker behind the 8. But that wouldn't be prudent here unless you were absolutely certain you could leave him safe. The majority of advanced players would try to move the 9, even if only a foot or so.)

The point to be made here is that, as in Eight-Ball, it is simply not necessary to run all the balls off the table in a single turn to win. Even though this game favors the better shotmakers, don't forget to use your head. Your shotmaking can always improve; your thinking should be optimal to begin with.

Getting Your Kicks

I can't teach you all there is to know about "kicking" (making contact with the lowest numbered ball by sending your cue ball to one or more rails first). There are so many ways to snooker and be snookered as to defy illustration; recognizing the angles of cue-ball flight available to you at any given time is so much a matter of judgment rather than pat answers.

We can examine the basics, though. Banking a ball, whether it's the cue ball or an object ball, is much like what your high-school geometry teacher used to call "bisecting the angle." If you place your cue ball opposite the second diamond on a long rail, aim it at the first diamond on the rail opposite, and strike it in its exact vertical center, you should successfully bank it into the nearest corner pocket. Place it in front of a side pocket and aim it at the second diamond (in either direction) on the opposite long rail, and you should see the same results.

Additionally, you'll learn from experience how to connect lines leading to corner pockets off a single rail, as shown in Diagram 148. Place the cue ball at the first diamond on the short rail, aim at the long-rail diamond nearest you (remember to aim at the diamond itself, not a point on the rail opposite the diamond) and shoot. Your cue ball should be in, or very close to, the diagonal, opposite corner pocket. The same is true if you begin at the short rail's second diamond and aim at the long rail's second diamond; ditto the third. And if you begin at a point in between those diamonds, parallel lines to those between the connecting first, second, and third diamonds will work equally as well.

Now with that information, it follows that by beginning at the short rail's first diamond and aiming somewhere *beyond* the long rail's first diamond, you can send your cue ball to a point on the far, short rail instead of the corner. If you aim at a point on the long rail short of its first diamond, your cue ball will take a diagonal path short of the opposite corner, and so on.

There is really no substitute for practicing this exercise with a cue ball and an object ball. See how many times in a row you can make contact, with various one-and two-rail routes. Add cue-ball English, and when you're comfortable with your progress, try making contact with one side of the object ball or the other. This exercise may sound tedious, but it's invaluable experience for Nine-Ball since "kicking" is largely a matter of judgment. (It will also help your Eight-Ball game in case your opponent has read this and is playing defense on you.)

How Would You Play This?

It's time to solve some of the game's typical problems. We can't possibly examine them all, but these are recurring situations, which call for you to think your way through rather than merely shoot balls into holes. A hint: these examples

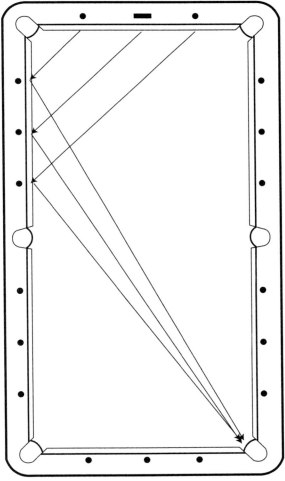

Diagram 148.

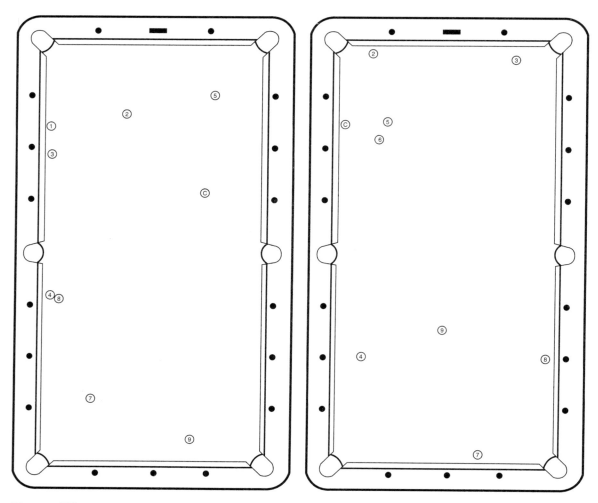

Diagram 149.   **Diagram 150.**

call for you to select the correct play, not necessarily to plan an out-right win.

In Diagram 149, you're being fooled again. You think you can pocket the 1-ball? What good does that do you, when there's no apparent way to get past the 4-8 combination? Drive the 1 out of there, killing the cue ball right at the point of contact, and while we're at it, hit the 1 hard enough to send it off three rails and, hopefully, into the 4-8. Separate those three balls and hook your opponent behind the 3, and he's in danger of losing the game.

Diagram 150 presents the "should I or shouldn't I?" dilemma. The 2-ball is not particularly hard to bank back into that corner nearest the 4, and if you make it you'll *probably* have shape on the 3 with the rest of the balls open. But that's too many probabilities. A smarter option would be to kick out the 2 and leave the cue ball on the end rail. If you get lucky and the 2 goes in someplace, you're right there with position on the 3. But if it doesn't go in someplace and you've utilized sufficient speed to send it down-table, the 5 and 6 are ideally positioned to block it from your opponent's view, and you're in the driver's seat again.

Diagram 151 is an example of going beyond the obvious. Even though you're generally encouraged to do whatever's simplest in pool, Nine-Ball is more likely than any other game to take away the possibility of simplicity. If you pocket the 1 in the obvious corner pocket, it's a virtual certainty your cue ball will run into the 3-ball, making position on the 2-ball impossible. In this case, you have your choice of two shots, both fairly tough, but both of which make far more sense than sinking the 1. (1) Drive the 1 out, leaving the cue ball behind the 3. (Again, as in Eight-Ball, object balls near a long rail and close to a pocket offer fertile snookering possibilities. By all means, apply your knowledge of the 90-degree rule to help you achieve this; it works just as well for balls you *don't* want to pocket as it does for balls you do. Visualize the *cue*-ball path you want from the 1-ball to the end rail, then work backward and visualize what the *object*-ball path must be to achieve that, assuming a center hit on the cue ball and appropriate speed. If you'd rather not use center ball, compensate accordingly. But even if you don't get the snooker, you'll at least have left distance between the cue ball and the object ball, with little chance of position on the 2 unless your

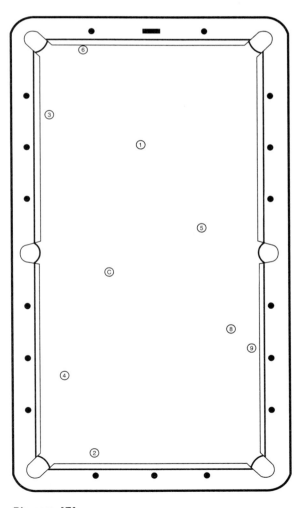

Diagram 151.

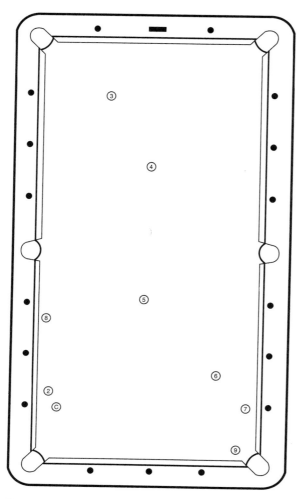

Diagram 152.

opponent turns the cue ball loose.) (2) Cut the 1-ball back into that pocket nearest the 3 with enough cue-ball speed to come around the table off three cushions for shape on the 2. The real secret to this shot is our friend inside English (high-left in the shot diagrammed). Aim the object ball not into the pocket itself, but about 4 inches short of the pocket (just past the 6-ball). Cue-tip deflection and spin take care of the rest; even if you miss, you should leave distance between the cue and 1-ball. Remember to use sufficient speed. This may feel uncomfortable at first—after all, it's not what you're used to shooting—but it should pay off.

I'm sure you're catching on by now, so Diagram 152 probably won't fool you; the shot is pretty clearly to play a billiard between the 2 and the 9. Cut the 2 thin in the direction of the 8 with some left-handed spin. The problem with this shot is that it doesn't drive the 2-ball very far away—the 8 will help see to that—and unless you sink the 9, you won't be leaving your opponent as safe as you want to. A much more enlightened shot selection is to drive your cue ball into the rail in front of the 2 to catch it thin. You now have a no-risk, three-way shot: You can make the 2-ball in the diagonal, opposite corner, you can pocket the 9 successfully on the billiard, and you can hook your opponent behind the 6 and/or 7, with distance between him and the 2 in any case.

One More Rack

In a final salvo of candor, I admit that there's not much I can do in a book to improve your ability to pocket balls. That's largely a matter of what coordination nature gave you and how much practice you're willing to undertake to apply your particular gifts to this particular game.

But I hope you're reasonably good at this game, at least good enough to sustain your enthusiasm and drive to improve. Like chess, pool has something new to teach you every time you play; *unlike* chess, not only do you have to grasp the concept, you have to execute it, too. And where concept and execution meet in pool is a magical place indeed, rich in wordless clues for you to uncover, hidden passageways for you to travel, and secret codes for you to crack. It's some game.

Some very, very good players never get around to seeing it that way, though; for them, the game is, and always will be, a simple matter of knocking balls into holes for cash.

That's their loss.

When talking about my love affair with the game over the years, I've become accustomed to describing myself as "ten times more fanatical than the most fanatical golf nut you know." You can fall well short of that level of enthusiasm—I would expect any rational person to do so—and still discover a lifetime friend in pool, I hope you do. When you get right down to it, I could hardly wish you more.

Index